Anthropology and Africa

Changing Perspectives
on a Changing Scene

Anthropology and Africa

Changing Perspectives on a Changing Scene

by Sally Falk Moore

The University Press of Virginia

Charlottesville and London

The University Press of Virginia
Copyright © 1994 by the Rector and Visitors
of the University of Virginia
First published 1994

Library of Congress Cataloging-in-Publication Data

Moore, Sally Falk, 1924–
    Anthropology and Africa : changing perspectives on a changing
scene / by Sally Falk Moore.
      p.   cm.
    Includes bibliographical references and index.
    ISBN 0-8139-1504-X. — ISBN 0-8139-1505-8 (pbk.)
    1. Ethnology— Africa— History.   I. Title.
GN308.3.A35M66   1994
301'.096— dc20   93-40047
                                             CIP

Printed in the United States of America

Contents

Contents

Preface

THIS BOOK is intended for people who are interested in Africa, in anthropology, in the history of ideas, or in all three. At present, there is no general short survey of the anthropology of Africa for someone wanting an overview of the field to consult or for use in a variety of courses. This volume is intended to fill that gap.

In the writing of this brief essay I have needed to control a desire to write detailed commentaries on the ethnographic contents and theoretical perspectives of many of the books mentioned. Much more could also have been said about the persons who devoted their lives to this field. Indeed, I am well aware of the vast materials over which I had to pass quickly. By necessity, I have omitted many authors and works altogether. But anyone who wants a substantial start in the anthropology of Africa will get a clear idea about previous scholarship and about what to read next from reading this work. I particularly hope that it will be read in Africa.

Some of my own interests and ideas have shaped this account and weighted it in particular ways. Other authors might have written different versions of the story, and no doubt they will. But this book will make the task easier for them; it covers the ground.

The idea for this project grew out of a chapter contributed to Robert Bates, ed., *Anthropology and the Disciplines* (1993). I am duly grateful. I would never have undertaken the labors involved if I had not first agreed to do that essay and then found the scope of a chapter too confining. The next version had better be a multivolume one!

Anthropology and Africa

Changing Perspectives
on a Changing Scene

Introduction

IN ITS HUNDRED YEARS of existence, social anthropology has been rethought and its approach reconstituted many times. To say that African studies have, at key moments, played a central role in these theoretical and methodological developments might be to understate the case. The fact that Africa itself has changed profoundly in the past century has been an important element in stimulating theoretical revision. Even as Africa was studied, it underwent a sequence of metamorphoses, repeatedly forcing anthropologists to rethink their project. Anthropology is at present more and more focused on understanding process over time rather than on what were once imagined to be fixed and perpetuated "traditions" and "customs." Thus, Africa has not only been the growing field for a bountiful harvest of studies of non-European cultural ideas and practices, but it has been increasingly a locale for the study of the dynamics of transformation.

Social anthropology was once described by Daryll Forde as the study of communities small enough to be treated as closed systems (referred to in Lienhardt 1976). The closed characterization would scarcely be appropriate today, and it has not been for decades. Moreover, the location of the "system," if any, is continually in question. No longer would any anthropologist conduct a local study in Africa without acknowledging the world beyond the community. The global political economy is in sight, even from the food gardens of the most peripheral of settlements. Intense local study is a method of investigation, not a definition of the anthropological problem. Today, a local study may still be small scale in geographical scope, but it must be large scale in conception.

The key method of social anthropology remains firsthand contact through fieldwork, but the anthropologist cannot but be intensely and constantly conscious of the larger world that surrounds the field site. After all, the anthropologist always comes from that other world even in those rare and valuable cases when the professional journey to the village is also a native's return. The use of a multiplicity of conceptual zoom lenses permits the anthropologist to focus on several distances at once. These simultaneous views of the near and the far have important epistemological consequences, and they pose two major practical and analytic challenges. The first is how to fit the local minutiae observed in fieldwork into larger politico-economic-cultural frames. The second is how to conceive the short term of field study as a segment of a longer temporal sequence. One is the problem of scale, the other the problem of history. These are ubiquitous and intertwined issues. They permeate the task of representation in ethnography. They can affect policy-making. They are fundamental to theory building.

A growing interdisciplinary dialogue has emerged from this place-time problematic since decolonization. Large-scale analysis has traditionally been the work of disciplines other than anthropology; hence, conversation with other academic fields has long loomed large on the anthropological agenda. Yet anthropology has been confident about the weight of its own contribution to these discussions. Given that innumerable localisms have more than local importance, the need to turn to local studies to understand the large scale seems obvious. The large scale is in many respects an aggregation of local systems. Only a knowledge of local affairs can demonstrate the causal dynamics that lie behind aggregate trends or can produce data on the range and effect of local variation. But the intellectual traffic goes both ways. The interpretation of local events is impoverished if it does not take adequate account of larger-scale economic, political, and cultural contexts. What is the connection between the rural village and the central government, the subsistence crop and the cash crop, the cultural conception of family and the reality of labor migration? Who makes famines and why? And what do the proselytizing world religions, Islam and Christianity, and the ideas propagated by Western medicine and Western education do to local systems of belief?

In the case of Africa, these are not merely peaceful questions about the design of academic research projects. The controversies imbedded in different understandings of the dynamics of scale are ingredients in a mix of incompatible conceptions of how society "works" that will pervade not only theoretical but political discourse in the next few decades. How much is the large-scale dynamic in fact the product of aggregate localisms? How much is large-scale organization an autonomous entity propelled by different forces from those found at the connecting points with the local level. How much can (or should) change be directed from the top? This task of analytic bridging, of making the connections and traveling intellectually among various levels of scale when addressing the question of causality (planned and unplanned) is increasingly seen as a major challenge to fin-de-siècle anthropology.

The second set of challenging tasks, closely related to the first, is those consequent on taking the time dimension into account. Social fields studied as moving, dynamic, living social entities observed in a state of propulsion within a trajectory of time are not the same entities that used to be inspected in anthropology's "tribal" and "culture pattern" days. Social/cultural anthropology was until a few decades ago a discipline founded on the notion of studying the customs of "traditional" groups, studying the presumably durable and repetitive patterns of thought and behavior that together formed cultural systems that could be compared. Societies could change. That went without saying. But for a long time in a certain kind of anthropology, it was not in their change but in their traditions that societies were thought most interesting. For a long time the reconstruction of a pure, untouched indigenous African system, as it might have been was more valued theoretically than present witnessing. The same anthropologists often produced both types of description, but in the old days, roughly from 1930 to 1960, the period when British social anthropology dominated African studies, only the reconstructions were valorized by the profession and used in theoretical comparisons.

A sharp distinction was generally made "between theoretical (i.e., sociological) understanding . . . and historical explanation" (Gulliver 1965, 83). But today, to conceive of observed social fields as potentially changeable entities that are continuously in motion, to focus on the spinning forward through time, sometimes repeating, sometimes shifting the shape of practice, poses entirely different methodological and interpretive questions than were even conceived in many earlier studies. "Historical" and "sociological" understandings are being combined. A reversal of priorities has been on its way for some time, privileging transformation as the central problematic, with continuity often reconceived as an interesting instance in which the possibility of transformation was successfully avoided.

These issues, then, underlie current general concerns in anthropological theory and practice, the matter of linking small-scale research to large-scale contexts, the reconception of fieldwork as the observation of current history in the making. Both raise the issue of causality in new terms and by implication pose questions about the power to consciously transform, or consciously reproduce, social forms. In Africa such questions are of more than theoretical interest. They have practical urgency.

Africa's ongoing economic, demographic, and political crises are critically serious, and some think them intractable (*Economist,* Sept. 25, 1993: 49–50). This cannot but be a major concern of academics in the decades to come, as it is of policymakers now. From unpayable national debts to AIDS, from famines to population explosions, from political violence to refugee camps, human suffering exists on a scale that is difficult to comprehend. For anthropologists, the study of Africa is consequently deeply entangled with the question of why, in so many places, the Africans they know firsthand live intermittently in such a variety of potentially desperate situations.

In the colonial period, anthropologists optimistically told

themselves and the world that if properly "used," their knowledge could ameliorate relations between government administrations and governed Africans. With decolonization the sense that this was an illusory hope became overwhelming, but that did not deter some from trying a newly constructive path. In the early postcolonial enthusiasm for "development," some anthropologists sought to advise the designers of economic expansion. The present, more pessimistic period has led to attempts to try to extract lessons from the failures and models from the successes; however, far more anthropologists are currently occupied with simply trying to understand what is (and was) occurring than are occupied with giving advice. In addition to every conceivable disaster, every imaginable social experiment is under way somewhere on the African continent. Some of these have been externally imposed by national and international agencies, some have been formed by ideology, and others have been created by the cumulative effect of individual practice.

Unless there continue to be academic centers for the training of Africanists both inside and outside of the continent, it is difficult to imagine how the many complex facets of the present situation will come to be understood, let alone repaired. The extremes and the variations are so numerous and so great that no social or intellectual issue exists that cannot be explored in an African context. Yet studies that promise intellectual gains but no immediate practical benefit are often attacked by those in the front lines of social reform. Public controversies over the benefits of "basic research" in Africa have periodically generated a degree of discomfort in a scholarly community that often feels helpless in the face of social disaster. The same attacks have generated a degree of critical self-consciousness that has enlivened anthropology and enlarged its theoretical and humane awareness.

Thus, it is now a commonplace that the very act of choosing a particular subject for analysis is likely to have implicit political significance. This idea has been especially forcefully applied to the writings of earlier generations that did their ethnographic work during the colonial period. But the notion that present work also has such implications is a less comfortable conception. Anthropologists currently working in Africa are as wary of offending the governments under whose shadow they labor as was an earlier generation. How that wariness informs the topics chosen for attention today and how it helps to identify the touchy subjects that have to be ignored is not much discussed in current print. The most acerbic political critique is always reserved for the times safely past.

Each new generation of anthropologists has thought of itself as transcending the crude misconceptions of an earlier group, as more aware of itself, as seeing the world more clearly. And some of that self-congratulation, though usually excessively larded with vanity, has been well founded. The very process of rejecting immediate antecedents and proposing alternative frameworks has propelled the field forward and given it a certain combative vitality. But old paradigms fortunately can be junked without destroying the literature in which they are imbedded. Thus, the retrospective reading of earlier works in African anthropology remains valuable. Ethnographies that are theoretically unacceptable often had as authors the only witnesses of a particular moment of local history. Although interpretations shift, the detailed observations on which they were based are irreplaceable. At the very least, present ethnographic work will serve that historical function in the future.

Thus, in an important sense, not only is social anthropology in a perpetual condition of paradigmatic transformation, in the Kuhnian manner, with temporarily dominant theoretical models ever replaced by newly ascendant ones, but over time the discipline has also filled its academic storehouse with a rich body of cumulative knowledge. There is no better example of this than the work that has been done in Africa. To be sure, data are always shaped by the models of the period that informed their collection. Much ethnographic observation was done with a keen eye, however, and there remains a durable core of moments witnessed and persons heard, of organization described and modes of thought recorded. Serious readers of

Introduction

old ethnographies know just how to look past the grand theory of the era of writing to glean only those harvests of information and understanding that speak to present concerns. It would be difficult to learn much about Africa without reading what anthropologists, past and present, have had to say about it. This review is principally concerned with the mainstream of French, British, and American anthropological work in Africa, although there have been substantial contributions from anthropologists in other countries, including Africans, Belgians, Dutch, Germans, and Japanese. (See Binsbergen 1982 on Dutch anthropology; Peek 1990 on Japan; contact the Pan African Anthropologists Association for the activities of present-day African anthropologists.) In the past there were only a few Africans in the profession. Their numbers are now increasing. Overall, however, the development of an Africanist anthropology has been largely in the hands of foreign anthropologists. Consequently, much of the anthropological chronicle of African culture and analysis of African society has been written in Anglo-European languages for an Anglo-European audience. This phenomenon is an important feature of the history traced in this volume, one that may well change in the future.

Anthropology and Africa: Beginnings

The Idea of Social Evolution and the Colonial Project

ANTHROPOLOGY did not come into existence as a formally recognized academic discipline until late in the nineteenth century. The initial preoccupations were two: to identify what was universal about all of humankind, despite its varied cultures, and to trace the evolution of human society through its successive stages, i.e., to put the evidence of cultural variation in a putative evolutionary order. Both projects required wide-ranging comparisons. Of necessity, the materials for broad comparison were found in the library, not in the field.

Of the "anthropological" scholars of the late nineteenth century, some had traveled and had brief contact with the exotic "others" they wrote about, but on the whole they relied on the writings of others, on observations made by missionaries and administrators and explorer-travelers. They used scattered facts from all over the world to illustrate their contention that all human beings had certain ideas and characteristics in common, and they also used the same kinds of scattered sources to illustrate a typology of different stages of social development. Disagreements existed about what the earliest and "original" forms were, what were independent inventions, and what had spread through diffusion, but whatever the disagreement about detail, in each dimension, the evolutionary account was conceived to culminate in the triumph of Western civilization, seen as the most advanced form of human society ever known.

The period at which this intellectual development emerged both preceded and coincided with the expanded Anglo-European colonization of Africa. For anthropology, this political fact eventually meant that access to an enormous domain of ethnographic knowledge would open up and that this access would exist under conditions set by the colonial presence. On the political plane as in the mission and in the agricultural estates of the colonies, the Europeans considered those they governed socially, culturally, morally, and technically "backward." Thus, evolutionary theory and the conception of nineteenth-century colonial administration as a civilizing mission resonated harmoniously with each other. But evolutionary theory did not represent the source of imperial expansion, nor did the colonial enterprise constitute the source of evolutionary theory. These were venerable political strategies and old ideas. The great empires of earlier historical periods had also enjoyed a similar rationale. What makes the nineteenth-century evolutionary and diffusionist models significant for the present account is that these grand conjectural reconstructions of a total human history became a central feature of intellectual discourse at the very beginnings of anthropology as a social science. The replacement of these grand totalizing schemes with the painstaking project of collecting evidence through fieldwork is the story of the coming of age of anthropology and of African studies within it.

From the start, the anthropological project was defined as the study of "others," of non-European peoples with other ways of life. The subject matter continued several much older streams in the British, European, and American intellectual traditions. It was nothing new to use a description of the way of life of "others" as an opportunity to make a commentary on Western society, sometimes only to extol its achievements and sometimes as an occasion to deplore its moral or political condition. In 1871 Tylor declared that anthropology was a reformer's science, entrusted with identifying in European culture the surviving traces of superstition, mistaken belief, and outmoded custom so that those vestiges of the past could be stamped out (1958, 2:539). In 1877 Morgan thought the Iroquois a model of morality and democracy and deplored the "career of property" and stratification in which the West was embroiled (Morgan 1963).

In the early days of this century, the assumption that it was the political fate of the Anglo-Euro-Americans to become the special observers and analysts of unfamiliar cultural traditions seemed to need no discussion, particularly because the others were not only the object of scholarly investigation, but were simultaneously the object of the "civilizing efforts" of missionaries and government administrations (Stocking 1987, 237). The most accessible examples for the Americans were the conquered Native American peoples; for the British and Europeans, the peoples of their colonies, Africans among them.

German writings about Africa, like those of the French and the British, began with the observations of missionaries, travelers, and administrators in the colonial territories. But German academic work on the subject ended early, when the Germans lost their African colonies at the end of World War I, and subsequently, when anthropological interests could not be pursued because of the racial and social theories of the Third Reich. By contrast, along with a stabilization of colonial control, British and French ethnological work in Africa expanded considerably from the 1920s and 1930s on. American anthropologists did not enter the African field in any numbers until very much later on.

Anthropology Professionalizes: New Standards of Evidence and New Criteria of Classification

A reaction against the speculativeness of the two early modes of classification— evolutionary and diffusionist— emerged when serious attempts to collect ethnographic evidence began. And from the intensification of that practical task emerged a major change of theoretical paradigm. Once the data began to be assembled in quantity, evolutionary and diffusionist categories were soon seen to be inadequate to the total labor of classification. One of the most dogged critics of these conjectural reconstructions was Franz Boas, the first American anthropologist and the dominant figure in the United States from 1896 to 1941. He taught generations of American anthropologists, including Melville Herskovits, America's first Africanist. Boas had been trained in the physical sciences and wanted to apply scientific evidentiary standards to anthropological research. His own fieldwork took place principally among the Native Americans of the Northwest coast of America, but he encouraged many of his students to work elsewhere.

One of the classifying frameworks that became a substitute for the evolutionary schemes was the culture-area concept, which first arose in American anthropology toward the end of the nineteenth century as a result of the need to devise a mode of categorizing an almost bewildering number of Native American cultures (Kroeber 1931; Wissler 1917). The culture area was a geographical unit in which there were a number of socially separate societies that nevertheless had certain cultural and environmental features in common. The most fundamental of these common features, and the one on which most culture-area classifications were founded, was a mode of production of food. The culture-area idea was a useful simplification, a way of building a general typology on the basis of some objective criteria, but it had its limitations. It was clear from the beginning that radically different cultures could exist in similar geographical environments, or similar ones could exist in different geographical settings. No single key was adequate for classification, let alone for explanation. But the culture-area concept was liberated from the question of evolution. It had no inherent need for ordering in terms of sequence, and it was closely tied to empirical data.

What is of interest for Africanists about this early framework of American anthropology is that in the 1920s Herskovits, who became the doyen of American Africanists, applied Wissler's idea of the culture area to the cultural map of Africa in his doctoral thesis (Herskovits 1926). In 1930 he published what became a famous paper, "The Culture Areas of Africa," in the journal *Africa* (see Dike 1963). He divided Africa into six areas, but he then reduced these into two categories, the dominantly pastoral and the dominantly agricultural. However imperfect, these attempts to make order out of ethnographic chaos, to separate evidence-based classification from any conjectural evolutionary or diffusionist scheme, represented a large step forward. The culture-area typology's firm grounding in economy gave an integrated core of earning-a-living realism to the classification and distinguished it from the bits-and-pieces approach of the diffusionists and the love of exotic details of the evolutionists. Applying the culture-area classification to African societies was quite a different enterprise from applying it to Native-American cultures. Native-American peoples had been conquered, often decimated, many of them moved from their lands and confined to reservations. With a few exceptions, their way of life had been radically changed by their defeat and displacement. They were a tiny minority in a land overwhelmingly dominated by the descendants of Anglo-Europeans. The sorting out of the culture areas of native North America was an act of historical reconstruction, closely tied to museum work and archeology. But Africa was a place in which the Anglo-Europeans constituted a tiny minority. Although the colonial period involved domination and forced change of many kinds, Africans retained viable societies that, although transformed by the advent of colonial rule, were not destroyed to the degree that most Native American societies had been. Many African rural economies continued long-established agricultural and pastoral practices. Indigenous languages and social and cultural frameworks, though profoundly affected by the colonial transformations, remained strikingly different from those of the Europeans. African Africa remained a going concern. Ethnological fieldwork in Africa would thus take place in an entirely different kind of milieu from that which existed in much of North America.

The years from 1920 to 1960 have been called the classic period of the growth of anthropology (Stocking 1987, 289). It was also the period in which ethnographic fieldwork in Africa came into its own. And for at least the last two of those decades, that very fieldwork was central to the formulation of the major theoretical perspectives of anthropology. This is particularly true of Anglophone anthropology. For the time that British social anthropologists dominated theory-building in social anthropology, that dominance was associated with models created from the African experience. Models of African "systems" were the central showpiece of British anthropological theorizing. The applicability or inapplicability of these models to other areas of the world, or indeed their utility for interpreting the African scene itself, eventually became the subject of lively critical writing and the stimulus for new theoretical invention. What is implied in the choice of 1960 as the terminal date of this era, that it was also the terminal date of the colonial period in many African countries. Postcolonial anthropology took new paths. To understand the special circumstances surrounding the outpouring of British studies in Africa during the late colonial period, it is useful to compare that flow with the much more limited work of French and American scholars in the same decades. The force of the subsequent reaction against British structural functional theory was proportionate to its earlier influence. African studies took a new turn, as did anthropology in general. Many of the eclectic theoretical frames now in use emerged from that period of critical discourse. Thus, African studies made several pivotal contributions to the direction and redirection of intellectual developments in anthropology.

In tracing the story of the place of African studies in the development of anthropology, one must remain aware of how small the numbers of social anthropologists were until well after the Second World War. "As late as 1939 there were only about twenty professional social anthropologists, in the modern sense, in the British Commonwealth" (Kuper 1973, 90). When studying African anthropology in the late forties, the student would find that "the Americans who had published on the basis of African fieldwork could be counted on the fingers of one hand: W. R. Bascom, E. Colson, J. H. Greenberg, and J. S. Harris." (McCall 1967, 27). As late as 1950 in all of the United States, only thirty-two anthropology courses were offered that concerned Africa, and only five focused exclusively on sub-Saharan Africa (Voegelin 1950, 387). At that time, of 820 universities in the United States, only about one-third offered any anthropology at all, only 25 had Ph.D. programs in the subject (ibid., 355). In 1950 there were fewer than five hundred American anthropologists, including archaeologists, physical anthropologists, and linguists as well as social/cultural anthropologists (ibid., 356–57). By the 1990s this number had increased more than tenfold. In 1950 all of the subfields together had ninety-four full professors. Thus, the intellectual audience for works in social/cultural anthropology has been far larger than the numbers of its practitioners might seem to warrant. African studies has, at various times, been a very important subfield of what was for a long time a small academic discipline, posing difficult questions, unsettling preconceived notions, providing the basis for new frameworks of analysis.

The major methodological change that took place as anthropology professionalized and grew was that it became more and more committed to intensive fieldwork and to the collection of empirical data. Protracted periods of close contact with the peoples being studied produced an entirely different kind of information from those bits and pieces that had been used in global evolutionary comparison and eventually led to an entirely different kind of analysis. But this change came slowly.

The Middle Colonial Period, 1920-40

Early Days: American and French Anthropologists in Africa

WITH A FEW EXCEPTIONS, anthropology in the United States was principally concerned with the native peoples of the Americas virtually until the end of World War II. Some ethnographic work was also done in the Pacific. Melville Herskovits, the one American anthropologist whose enthusiastic interest centered on Africa, has already been mentioned. He was to become the teacher of most of the next generation of Americans who worked in Africa. It was largely through Herskovits's early efforts that African studies eventually came into its own in the United States. He and his wife spent five months in Abomey in Dahomey in the 1930s and in 1938 published a two-volume study, *Dahomey, an Ancient African Kingdom.* But Herskovits was not only occupied with Africa's past. He had a strong sense of the importance of studying change in Africa. Thus, on the eve of independence, together with W. R. Bascom, he edited an influential book entitled *Continuity and Change in African Cultures* (1959). Herskovits's major influence was not so much through any achievements as a field-worker as through his indefatigable lecturing, publishing, and teaching about Africa and the African diaspora and through his considerable organizational skill in building at Northwestern University "the leading center of African Studies in the U.S." (Dike 1963, 2). But despite Herskovits's great energy, not until the 1950s was his interest shared by enough scholars in a variety of disciplines in the United States to make possible the founding of an American organization, the African Studies Association, started in 1957. Its first president was, of course, Melville Herskovits, "not merely a pioneer, but a scholarly figure of exceptional force, a prolific writer and an indefatigable traveler" (Southall 1983, 64). In the new association, "of the forty-eight founding fellows, ten were anthropologists," (ibid., 63). Thus, as is evident from that start, a participation in the organized scholarly world of African studies had two marked effects on American anthropology. One was to commit anthropologists to ongoing interdisciplinary contact, and the other was to further internationalize American anthropology, because French and British anthropologists had long preceded most of the Americans into Africa.

A. R. Radcliffe-Brown, whose theoretical work was later to dominate British social anthropology for nearly two decades, also contributed to this internationalization of young American scholars. He taught at the University of Chicago for several years beginning in 1931. Through him several Americans met British anthropologists; for example, Lloyd Fallers was sent to A. I. Richards, by then the director of the East African Institute of Social Research, and she provided him with assistance in making contacts for his fieldwork. Other Americans who received training in Britain and did fieldwork in Africa in the early years included Hortense Powdermaker, Paul and Laura Bohannan, and Alfred and Grace Harris (McCall 1967, 28).

In France the pioneers were Maurice Delafosse and Marcel Griaule (for a description and appreciative critique of their work, see Clifford 1988, 55–91). Delafosse was a colonial officer with many years of service in West Africa who later undertook a second career, that of teaching at the Ecole Coloniale and the Institut d'Ethnologie. He trained many colonial officers in ethnographic method and became the first professor of Black African languages at the Ecole des Langues Orientales. "After Delafosse's death [in 1926] the principal influence on the first generation of professional fieldworkers in France was exerted by another charismatic teacher, Marcel Mauss" (ibid., 61–62). In African studies, there is no question that the principal French anthropologist for at least two decades after the 1930s was Marcel Griaule. His major achievement and that of his "school" was an extraordinary set of works on the Dogon of what is now Mali (Griaule 1948; Griaule and Dieterlen 1965). The early journeys Griaule led to West Africa were strongly oriented toward museum work. Many artifacts were assembled, photographs, maps, and recordings made, and documents brought back to France. Later Griaule's ethnographic interests focused more and more on Dogon thought, on the meaning of ritual, myth, and symbol. His larger objective, beyond the Dogon, was to distill the essence of West African philosophies and religion. How much the product of this endeavor was actually an African vision and how much Griaule's remains in debate.

> Over time he established, to his own satisfaction, the exis-
> tence of a ramified but coherent culture area he later por-
> trayed as one of three major divisions of sub-Saharan Africa:
> the Western Sudan, Bantu Africa, and an intermediate zone
> in Cameroon and Chad. Each region was characterized by a
> traditional sophie or science— a mode of knowledge in-
> scribed in language, habitat, oral tradition, myth, technol-
> ogy, and aesthetics. Griaule discerned common principles
> underlying the three African epistemological fields, and this
> permitted him to use the Dogon and their neighbors as priv-
> ileged examples of l'homme noir— microcosms of "African"
> thought, civilization, philosophy, and religion. A characteris-
> tic movement from parts to wholes to more inclusive wholes
> was Griaule's basic mode of ethnographic representation.
> (Clifford 1988, 57)

Copans (1977, 23) says of Griaule's idealism, "The mind accounts for and is the basis of the social concept and African societies are worthy of interest because their spiritual forthcomings are quite the equal of 'ours' (of Christianity, obviously). To this idealism is added an ideological vision of the colonial phenomenon as a boon or blessing."

Griaule's interpretive preoccupation with the "essence" of African systems of philosophy and modes of knowledge, his willingness to generalize very broadly about "the African" from limited comparative data, and his mode of collecting field material by having the Dogon stage rituals for the camera and by extracting exegeses from his informants through aggressive interrogation turned out not to be a particularly exportable style of ethnographic work and interpretation. Clifford comments that "French fieldwork has never assumed a distinct identity and has, in effect, been invisible to anthropologists of other traditions" (1988, 65).

The Colonial Context and British Social Anthropology: The 1920s and 1930s

The opposite was true of British fieldwork in Africa in the 1930s— it had deep methodological and theoretical effects on anthropology for many decades. Three factors together produced the dominant style of the British Africanists. One was the professional commitment to lengthy, intensive periods of fieldwork with a focus on social and political relationships. The second was the existence of a prevalent theoretical model, the functionalist or structural-functionalist approach. To compress it crudely, this analytic framework postulated that all of the contemporaneous cultural and social features of a stable society could be assumed to form part of a coherent and interdependent system. The task of the interpreter was to infer the connections. The third factor was the historical context, the British colonial situation in Africa.

The self-definition of British colonial policy in Africa was that it would operate by means of "indirect rule." Local government should, wherever possible, be carried on through indigenous political institutions. This assumed the existence of self-governing tribes as the underlying units of native political organization. The enunciation of this plan for African government is associated with Sir Frederick Lugard, the first governor of British Nigeria (1914–19). Obviously, the process of ruling "through" African organizations deeply changed the nature of local structures and the conditions of their existence, even where indigenous forms appeared to be retained.

What were the implications for anthropology? The policy of formally delegating power to native authorities and native courts made knowledge of African political and legal institutions an important prerequisite of colonial administration. Anthropologists thought of themselves as useful and expert in the study of such societies. The government sometimes agreed and used anthropologists for the collection of information or even occasionally in administrative roles. But in general there was a strong preference for using local political officers for these purposes whenever possible. Lackner (1973, 134, 136) quotes Lugard and another official report to this effect. For one thing, many administrative officers were needed, and there were very few trained anthropologists. For another, the official view was that it was usually easier and more efficient to teach anthropology to a British political officer than it was to put up with the peculiar ways of anthropologists whose interests were not always congruent with those of the administration.

Some administrative officers were interested in anthropology and were given special opportunities to make extensive ethnographic investigations. Several (Talbot 1915, 1923, 1926, 1932; Rattray 1923, 1929; Meek, 1925, 1931, 1937) were seconded for various periods as "government anthropologists" (Forde 1953, 843). There was certainly a good deal of government ambivalence about anthropology. The sense prevailed that a great deal of the information that professional anthropologists were given to collecting, from proverbs to accounts of rituals, from myths to recipes for herbal medications, did not directly relate to the practical problems of administration. And there were times when anthropologists might even be thought a subversive influence on the indigenes.

Undeterred by these attitudes, however, anthropologists would have preferred to be seen as useful. The profession certainly was sorely in need of more opportunities for research and of sources of financial support. In London, the profession tried intermittently to persuade the government that anthropology could indeed help in the affairs of colonial rule. The Royal Anthropological Institute made representations to that effect from early on in the century (Lackner 1973, 138–42). By the mid-1920s the nature of the interface between scholarly and administrative interests in Africa had become clearer. The scholars saw themselves as increasing the body of knowledge of Africa, as informed spokesmen for the point of view of the African, and as intermediaries between the interests of the indigenes and the objectives of the administrators when there were difficulties. But until after the Second World War, "although the resources in men and funds devoted to anthropological study and teaching . . . were exiguous in the extreme and such studies did not receive any significant support from colonial administrations, the influence of academic anthropology did to some extent filter throughout the administrative services through contacts with the universities and with the Royal Anthropological Institute, of which many of the more scholarly administrators became Fellows." (Forde 1953, 843, 844, cites a long list of these and notes some of their many publications.)

Despite the fact that the anthropologists came from the dominant society, they were preoccupied with the dominated population, its affairs, and its well-being. Anthropologists mixed freely with the Africans among whom they worked, often living among them, acknowledging no color bar and respecting none of the many social boundaries between rulers and ruled that were conventional among white administrators and settlers. Thus, very often, "the very existence of social anthropology in the colonial period constituted a source of potential radical criticism of the colonial order itself" (James 1973, 42), but the form of expression of that criticism had to be indirect. Anthropologists could not possibly mount a direct political attack on the colonial enterprise and continue to work in the colonies, even as it is impossible today for anthropologists to openly criticize the post-colonial governments whose permission they need to carry on their research. The relationship was not without its political complexities.

> As an individual, the anthropologist can often appear as a critic of colonial policy, of the philosophy of western superiority upon which it was based and in terms of which it was justified: and he was usually at odds with the various administrators, missionaries, and other local Europeans he had

dealings with. He cannot often be seen unambiguously as a willing agent of colonialism. But he was nevertheless dependent upon colonial authorities for permission to carry out his studies, and sometimes for material support; and in the inter-war period at least, open political dissent was scarcely possible within colonial society. An anthropologist who turned out to be anything more than a mild social embarrassment could scarcely have been tolerated; and thus, for anthropology to continue at all, appearances of co-operation had to be kept up. (Ibid.)

The complex intertwinings between the needs of colonial administration and the interests of anthropologists and other scholars of Africa was epitomized in the affairs of the International Institute of African Languages and Cultures, which was founded in 1926. The institute was launched with funding from the Rockefeller Foundation, the Carnegie Foundation, and some colonial governments, and Lord Lugard was made the head of its executive council (Feuchtwang 1973, 83). The institute's five-year plan for itself was modeled on an article Bronislaw Malinowski had published in *Africa,* "Practical Anthropology" (1929; Feuchtwang 1973, 83). The institute had "the express aim of achieving a closer association between scientific knowledge and research and the interests of African peoples, colonial governments, and other European agencies in African territories" (Forde 1953, 847). The study of culture contact and social change was envisioned as a prominent part of its work from the beginning.

The International African Institute (IAI) journal, *Africa,* published articles by anthropologists, administrators, and colonial educationists "concerning both the broader aspects and particular instances of social change in relation to governmental action" (ibid., 848). Forde, who became Director of the IAI after World War II, said that in the long run this scholarly concern with social change "contributed to the creation of a climate of opinion concerning the need to give greater responsibility to Africans in the development of the new social structures that must inevitably follow from increasing participation in the world economy" (ibid., 848, 849). What is clear is that the various phases of the colonial period involved different conceptions of the administrative project and some shifts in the role of the anthropologist. Anthropologists increasingly involved themselves in African social research and development work as a form of applied anthropology, both in rural and in urban areas. During the Second World War and thereafter, this kind of effort and the social science research associated with it accelerated its tempo. More administrators recognized that practical problems were not easily addressed without "basic ethnographic field investigation" (ibid., 853).

These connections between anthropology and the colonial enterprise became the subject of considerable invective in the 1960s and 1970s. Thus the "colonial connection" became a political issue among "radical" internal critics of anthropology just at the point at which such connections no longer had any practical relevance, i.e., in a postcolonial reaction. Other attacks came from African academics who wanted to repossess control of scholarship concerned with their own societies. This invective went on for decades. As Rabinow (1986) has said of the 1980s, "contemporary academic proclamations of anti-colonialism . . . must be seen as political moves within the academic community. Neither Clifford nor any of the rest of us is writing in the late 1950s. His audiences are neither colonial officers nor those working under the aegis of colonial power. Our political field is more familiar: the academy in the 1980s" (252). The negative mention of colonialism in a text today is a wholly safe form of politically correct self-certification by the author.

Apart from the vituperation of the 1960s and 1970s, which often became as drearily conventionalized as the vulgarized conceptual straw men it attacked, there was in addition considerable serious questioning of the models on which so much of anthropological theory had been founded. The ahistoricity and selective constructions of the structural-functional paradigm became strikingly clear. The "colonial period mentality" critique represented one dimension of the more general proposal that a new set of problematics be addressed.

The fundamental questions to be asked about anthropology in the colonial context do not so much concern the practical role of applied anthropology in the colonial period, which, all told, probably was seldom damaging to Africans. The more important and difficult questions concern the extent to which a general perception of the colonial world was shared by all concerned— anthropologists, colonial administrators, and the home government and public. To what extent did anthropology share in the general discourse about Africa? Was it usually carried on in terms of common concepts about the nature of "advanced" societies and "backward" societies? How much were the conflictual issues implicit in the relationship between dominant and subordinate peoples avoided as academic topics? Is anthropology in any sense an autonomous intellectual field?

A full history of the many facets of the African studies controversies of the 1960s and 1970s has yet to be written. The categorical terms within which the academic fights over these issues took place were surely just as deeply entangled with the larger politics of the immediate postcolonial decades as was the anthropology of the colonial period interwoven with the colonial situation. Both frameworks now look very much out of date.

As for the functionalist paradigm, the theoretical use made of it to reject evolutionism and to emphasize the integrated social wholeness, indigenous morality, and logical coherence of African society and thought was seen by anthropologists of the time as a way of valorizing those cultures for a Western audience. The "closed system" version of functionalism associated with A. R. Radcliffe-Brown tended to focus the scholarly interests of field-workers on producing "pure" editions of the native cultures they were describing. The interesting question for them was how these societies "functioned" before colonial intervention. The British social anthropologists sought to discover what the native traditions had been when they were "intact," uncorrupted by contact with the West. This conception of African social systems as separate and independent units that once functioned as coherent and integrated social wholes fits neatly with the political conception of the "tribe" used by the colonial administration to divide up the population it governed into intelligible units.

How could the conception of African peoples actually observed in the midst of vast social changes envisioned by Malinowski and the IAI plan be reconciled with the conception of "unspoiled" indigenous tribal systems so prominent in anthropological theory and ethnographic description? That apparent contradiction held no intellectual difficulties for its proponents. The structural-functional model could be preserved by postulating two broad types of coherent social systems, the tribal and the modern-industrial. The complex reality that was actually visible in Africa was conceived to be neither one nor the other; rather, it was assumed to be transitional. Somehow the tribal would eventually become the modern, and the African cultures that were currently disrupted would ultimately be replaced.

Thus, a third category, temporally marked as an intermediate phase, was postulated as the contemporary condition. The intermediate phase was seen as noncoherent and full of conflicting norms and values. The "original" tribal systems were assumed to have been integrated functioning wholes. Modern systems also were assumed to be coherent functioning totalities. All the parts of each type fit together and functioned as contributions to the life of the whole (Radcliffe-Brown 1952, 181). But in this paradigm until the disrupted tribal could become modern it was bound to be made up of functionally nonreconcilable parts drawn from two world, hence deeply troubled and conflicted (Wilson and Wilson [1945] 1968).

Professional Fieldwork and the Era of Malinowski

In 1927 Bronislaw Malinowski was appointed to the first chair in anthropology at the University of London (London

School of Economics), where he had already taught on and off for several years. He was no Africanist, but he was to have many students who were, and his influence on them was profound. Until 1938, when he left Britain, Malinowski was unquestionably the major figure in the London anthropological scene. His seminar was widely attended, not just by students at the LSE but also by students from other programs. Max Gluckman, for one, regularly commuted from Oxford to participate.

Malinowski's was an overwhelming personality, and that fact combined with his remarkable ethnographic writings on the Trobriand Islands to inspire his students. The superb quality of his fieldwork and the uses of it he made in argument changed the course of professional anthropology. The collection and interpretation of a large body of detailed material on all aspects of one society, including careful descriptions of the mundane aspects of daily life, was a startling innovation.

In a series of monographs published in the 1920s and 1930s, Malinowski presented the exotic Trobriand way of life as an integrated, logical whole. His approach sharply contrasted with late-nineteenth-century writers, Tylor and Frazer and others, whose grand generalizations were never about one society but about stages in the thought and technological achievement of humankind. The evolutionists' arguments were constructed out of selected bits of evidence of like customs found around the world. Tylor would, in a single page, illustrate a contention by citing similar practices of Africans, Eskimos, Hawaiians, European villagers in the Middle Ages, and any number of other peoples. Tylor built his arguments topically and then illustrated them with scattered examples to show the commonalities of the human imagination in comparable circumstances. In contrast, Malinowski drew on his vast knowledge of the Trobriand Islands to build a picture of a single total system in which the indigenous institutions of economy, kinship, religion, politics, and law intersected in complementary ways. Malinowski's many monographs, written on the basis of his two years' stay in the islands, provided students with an eloquent demonstration of the kinds of field material he considered it essential to gather.

Before Malinowski came along, the few detailed ethnographies of African peoples that existed had been written by missionaries, including Henry A. Junod's *The Life of a South African Tribe* (1912), E. W. Smith and A. Dale's *The Ila-Speaking Peoples of Northern Rhodesia* (1920), and Bruno Gutmann's *Das Recht der Dschagga* (1926). These were remarkable works, but they were strongly skewed by the proselytizing interests, special roles, and related preconceptions of their authors, who also tended to rely heavily on the accounts of a limited number of informants rather than on observation. There were also a few monographs commissioned by colonial governments, such as those by Northcote Thomas on the Ibo and then on the Timne (1913–14), Rattray on the Ashanti (1923, 1929) and Meek in Nigeria (1937), but as Evans-Pritchard commented about them, "It must be said . . . that even at their best the writings of these administrator-anthropologists seldom satisfy the professional scholar" (1962, 111).

By contrast, Malinowski's work set a very high professional standard. Living among the matrilineal Trobrianders for two years, speaking their language, talking with them about anything and everything, watching the daily round of activities, he gathered an astounding amount of material. From the planting of gardens to the building of canoes, from ritual to law, from ideal norms to actual practices, he explored everything that presented itself and asked about the rest. No similar wealth of detail about one people had been attempted or achieved by a professional anthropologist before. Thus, for example, Malinowski's teacher and later colleague at the London School of Economics, C. G. Seligman, had been on several major field expeditions around the world from the time of the Torres Straits expedition of 1898–89 and had done the kinds of investigations that up to then had passed as fieldwork. Seligman's African study in this mode was the "compendious" *A Survey of the Pagan Tribes of the Nilotic Sudan* (with B. Z. Seligman, 1932; for a brief comment on Seligman see Lienhardt 1976, 182).

Seligman's student, Malinowski, changed the character of fieldwork. His method redefined the anthropological project: it became the intensive study of a small community. That Malinowski also built a functionalist rationale for this type of fieldwork added a theoretical dimension. As he saw it, the small-scale society was not just the physical unit of study for practical reasons, it was the theoretically defined totality in which the functions of institutions and their integration within a cultural whole could be demonstrated.

Not only did a number of those who participated in Malinowski's seminar at the LSE in the 1930s do their fieldwork in Africa, but a particular subgroup of these eventually came to control major departments of social anthropology in Britain. The group included a number of women who later had distinguished professional careers. At various stages, Africanist participants in the Malinowski seminar included E. E. Evans-Pritchard, Audrey Richards, Hilda Kuper (then Beemer), Isaac Schapera, Phyllis Kaberry, Hortense Powdermaker, Meyer Fortes, S. F. Nadel, Gordon Brown, Max Gluckman, Ellen Hellmann, Godfrey Wilson and Monica Hunter (later Wilson) (A. Kuper 1973, 90–92, 154–57; Brown 1973, 187).

Malinowski's own interest in Africa was considerable from early on in his career of teaching at the LSE. That interest intensified over the years, and Africa figured in expanding his theoretical views. It presented a practical and theoretical situation that Malinowski had not addressed in his Trobriand work. Africa was a place of enormous social change, both directed and spontaneous. Malinowski responded to this evident fact by arguing that transformations could and should be studied. He also argued that anthropological knowledge might have some practical use in Africa. Malinowski (1929, 1930) conceived of anthropologists as able to supply administrators with objective information about African ways of life that would prevent colonial governments from making serious errors of policy out of ignorance of indigenous culture. He was especially concerned with policies that might be damaging to Africans and angrily criticized both the record of violence that had been perpetrated against Africans by colonial administrations and less lethal but nevertheless damaging blunders in the ongoing matter of land tenure policy. Malinowski's strong Africa-related interest in social change and in applied anthropology shows that he saw no problem in reconciling a "functional" approach to "traditional" society with the study of changing society.

The monographs written by participants in his seminar did not always confine themselves to analyses of the "traditional." Thus, Monica Hunter's *Reaction to Conquest* (1936), "a study of the Pondo not only in their 'tribal' setting, but also as labourers on European farms and in the towns of South Africa, has been singled out as a notable example of a diachronic or historically-dimensioned study at a time when ahistorical and static studies are said to have dominated the field" (Brown 1973, 187).

Although Malinowski did not himself do any fieldwork in Africa, he was in contact with what became the International African Institute virtually from its founding in 1926 and in 1934 visited the continent for several months. At that time he attended a conference in South Africa and also went to see his student, Hilda Beemer, where she was working in Swaziland. He also visited Audrey Richards (see 1939, 1940, 1955, 1959, 1967), who was then working among the Bemba, and stopped off on Kilimanjaro, where he made contact with Chief Petro Itosi Marealle, who had published some ethnographic materials on the Chagga. Malinowski's interest in Africa must also have been intensified by his contact with African students in London, whose views of the colonial experience must have been quite different from that of the colonial office. Jomo Kenyatta, for one, was in Malinowski's seminar, and Malinowski wrote the introduction to his ethnography of the Kikuyu, *Facing Mount Kenya* (1938).

The Later Colonial Period to 1960

The 1940s and 1950s: Radcliffe-Brown, Evans-Pritchard, and Fortes

I N 1937 A. R. Radcliffe-Brown moved from the University of Chicago to Oxford and soon replaced Malinowski as the central figure in British social anthropology (Kuper 1973, 65). Like Malinowski, Radcliffe-Brown was another influential non-Africanist who later had a major impact on African studies. Born in 1881, he had many years of experience behind him before he took up his Oxford post. His fieldwork, done among the Andaman Islanders from 1906 to 1908, was as old-fashioned in method as Malinowski's had been innovative. The same could be said of his Australian fieldwork. "His work among the Australian aborigines, in 1910–12 . . . was survey work of the kind practised by Rivers or Seligman" (ibid., 57). But his Australian period produced a massive comparative study of the formal kinship and categorical structures of Australian aborigines. This oeuvre, although heavily based on the research of others, not only organized what had been a mass of jumbled evidence into an intelligible order but also used it to address analytical issues. This was Radcliffe-Brown's métier, and he ultimately made his own framing of comparative questions the dominant issues in anthropology for a decade.

Radcliffe-Brown's theoretical constructs, to which he devoted himself fully after his early forays into fieldwork were completed, were often recognizably built on Durkheim's works, particularly *The Rules of Sociological Method* (1962) and *The Elementary Forms of the Religious Life* (1961). From *The Rules of Sociological Method* Radcliffe-Brown derived the proposition that anthropology was a comparative sociology that should be devoted to the discovery of social laws, which were cultural regularities. These could be discovered through comparison and classification. From *The Elementary Forms of the Religious Life* Radcliffe-Brown borrowed his emphasis on the importance of groups and on the way group solidarity was both constituted by and represented in a common stock of cultural norms. He stressed that all customs and rules were to be understood as a contribution to the social life of the whole (Radcliffe-Brown 1952, 181). Societies were presumed to be integrated social systems in which anthropologists sought to identify and explain the connections among seemingly disparate practices. Cultural comparison could demonstrate the validity of these associations by showing that they recurred in different societies. Radcliffe-Brown's structural functionalism provided a framework that not only opened a theoretical place for new fieldwork findings but invited comparisons.

A tremendous flow of innovation in social anthropology followed from the late 1930s to 1950s. It gained momentum from three temporal conjunctions: Radcliffe-Brown's arrival at Oxford in 1937 and his need for comparative ethnographic data to put his ideas into practice; a concurrent outpouring of the results of field research done in Africa in the previous decade; and the eventual presence in every major anthropology department in Britain of one or another of a group of bright, creative, young Africanists. The fact that the Africanists all knew one another and all worked within a general framework of common assumptions gave a remarkable impetus to their creativity. They were not all alike by any means, and they had some theoretical differences, but they all did very detailed fieldwork in the Malinowskian tradition, and they were all interested in presenting and comparing their findings and in developing the field theoretically. Their basic assumption was that there were logical reasons for the structures of African societies and that those could be discovered. The Africanists at Oxford, Cambridge, London, and eventually Manchester constituted a ready-made, informed audience for each others' work and ideas. Not only were they all active in each other's seminars and in the International African Institute in London, but they were in close communication with colleagues in the research institutes in Africa— the East African Institute of Social Research in Uganda (first headed by Audrey Richards and later by Lloyd Fallers and Aidan Southall) and the Rhodes-Livingstone Institute in Northern Rhodesia (first led by Godfrey Wilson and later by Max Gluckman and eventually by Elizabeth Colson and Clyde Mitchell). Indeed, some of them did research under these auspices.

Theory linked each individual's specialized ethnographic work to a larger whole. Theory-building became the medium of engagement in intellectual contact and the rationale for constant communication. The effect was synergistic. African studies surged and so did theory-building in anthropology. Particular works of this period illustrate how the originality of individuals and the momentum of the group combined to produce a remarkable series of analyses.

In 1937 E. E. Evans-Pritchard published his pathbreaking book about a people of the Sudan, *Witchcraft, Oracles, and Magic among the Azande.* The effect on all subsequent discussions of witchcraft and religion in Africa was so great as to be incalculable. Evans-Pritchard demonstrated the intellectual logic that lay behind Zande beliefs. He showed that these tenets were not a miscellaneous scattering of disparate notions but rather a systematic set of ideas about the social causality of misfortune by breaking with previous ethnographic conventions in which magical and mystical ideas were reported as lists of disconnected, irrational beliefs. Instead, Evans-Pritchard showed how the Zande used these ideas in their daily lives. They applied the same logic to witchcraft and magic that they did to their practical affairs, assuming that "mystical" forces operated in the same way as objective physical forces. Given these premises, the logic was unassailable and, as a form of reasoning, no different from any practical, instrumental mode of thought. If one proceeds from the premise that there are few if any accidents, that thoughts and actions in the social universe can affect physical events, that ill-will is the likely source of mystical harm-doing, then in any particular case the question becomes one of determining whether witchcraft caused a particular misfortune. The Zande consulted powerful oracles for the answer and then put magical countermeasures into action both for self-protection and for vengeance. If someone died subsequently, that was prima facie proof that the person had been the witch and the countermeasures had succeeded.

On the basis of much less adequate, much earlier ethnographic reports, previous interpretations, such as those of the French philosopher Lucien Lévy-Bruhl, had used witchcraft ideas to argue that there were two quite different forms of thought, the "prelogical mentality" of primitives, and the logical mentality of moderns (1910). Instead, Evans-Pritchard demonstrated in great detail that if one could show the premises on which the Zande operated and the use that they made of their mystical beliefs in their lives the consistency and logic of the system would emerge and did not differ from the logic used in practical affairs anywhere. Evans-Pritchard's contentions were consciously and intentionally directed as a counterargument to the two-modes-of-thought views of Lévy-Bruhl (Evans-Pritchard 1937; see also Douglas 1981, 27–31). The debate about the nature of rationality and about the simultaneous existence in any society of multiple realities and a multiplicity of modes of thought continues to simmer (see, for example, Tambiah 1990), but the explanatory territory conquered by Evans-Pritchard's Azande work has never been retaken. It stands as a major ethnographic and conceptual contribution to anthropological theories of knowledge.

Evans-Pritchard worked at Oxford under Radcliffe-Brown and from 1939 to 1941 was joined by Meyer Fortes. The three of them generated a number of major works in the years of their most intense contact. Thus, in 1940 Fortes and Evans-Pritchard edited a pathbreaking comparative volume called *African Political Systems*. In the Radcliffe-Brownian mode, it sought to classify African systems into two types, those with centralized systems of rule and those without. Both Evans-Pritchard and Fortes had done ethnographic work among peoples with segmentary lineage systems; hence, their preoccupation was to explain the ways in which politics functioned in societies without centralized government. This was a body of new data and a new analysis. Thus, in the same year Evans-Pritchard published two more monographs on peoples of the Anglo-Egyptian Sudan, *The Nuer* (1940a) and *The Political System of the Anuak* (1940b), and Fortes was hard at work on his two major monographs on the Tallensi of Ghana, *The Dynamics of Clanship among the Tallensi* (1945) and *The Web of Kinship among the Tallensi* (1949b). In the Nuer book, Evans-Pritchard's interest in African modes of thought is as evident as it was in the work on the Azande. Either he took a Western concept, such as that of time, and addressed the variety of ways in which the Nuer conceived it or he took a Nuer word that had no direct translation into English and elucidated its various referents. These two themes in his work— the interest in political group organization and structure and the interest in modes of thought— stimulated many other scholars to work along these lines. A third theme in his work, the conviction that history is an essential part of anthropology, now has much currency in anthropology. That theme appeared in Evans-Pritchard's publication of a historical book, *The Sanusi of Cyrenaica* (1949).

Although Fortes had been a psychologist before becoming an anthropologist and also had an interest in African ideas and religions and although his Tallensi monographs were surely strongly stimulated by Radcliffe-Brown's theoretical interests, he constructed substantial theoretical frameworks of his own. Fortes was preoccupied with lineage structure and strongly stressed the norms of kinship among the Tallensi, the ties of relationship, and the nature of obligation, but he did not neglect the political structuring of alliances and enmities among and between clans, to which he devoted one of his books. Both Fortes and Evans-Pritchard addressed the large-scale political structuring of noncentralized societies and not only the domestic domain of kinship. The intellectual context of this work and its striving for generalization can be seen in the preoccupation with comparison in the collection of papers entitled *Afri-*

can Systems of Kinship and Marriage (1950) edited by Radcliffe-Brown and Daryll Forde. Some of the theoretical constructs of the 1940s have been refined and elaborated since they were originally proposed, and others have been challenged and discarded, but in their time they represented part of a rich effusion of careful ethnography and bold interpretation. Their authors built out of it a field of theoretical discourse in anthropology that has had continuing cogency.

Fortes wanted to distill from his ethnographic work the key characteristics of lineage-based social organization (1970). Many of the categories whose implications he elaborated became for a time part of the conventional tool kit of anthropology. Today it is difficult to remember that many of these matters were by no means spelled out when Fortes came on the scene. In some of its dimensions, his model was normative, a picture of repetitive patterns, a set of rules that governed the kinship order. In his other modes of description, his analytic framework was more dynamic. For example, he emphasized that among the Tallensi, kinship constituted a social field within which the tensions between ties of parentage and ties of marriage were played out and that at the larger-scale level of corporate social relations analogous polar tensions existed (1949b, 341). Although stated as if this were a set of simple ethnographic facts, such ideas were very much Fortes's inferences about the systematic way particular contradictory pulls and loyalties operated to create tensions and bonds within the fields of Tallensi social organization.

Nevertheless, in his other voice, Fortes had no doubt that Tallensi kinship structure was "a coherent system" (ibid., 343) and that it had "standard forms" that could be identified (ibid., 11). Fortes's normative, system-oriented approach was in these respects in keeping with the thought of his period. His writings on kinship contain many examples of reified interpretations; however, his own experiential awareness that the realities were more complex often breaks through. "In considering the incidence of jural or ritual rights and duties, or in determining the scope of kinship sentiments, we cannot always lay down exact limits within which they apply" (ibid., 10). Thus, surprises of detail in his rich ethnographies reward careful reading.

Fortes did not shy away from describing facts that did not fit the model of the tribe. Thus, in sketching the extent of Tallensi society, he did not simply refer to a neatly bounded entity that might have satisfied colonial administrative criteria but instead explained that he was in reality dealing with a dispersed and diversely interconnected system of alliances, kin relationships, and common performances of ritual that linked many settlements with varying degrees of intensity.

Thus, among the most interesting of Fortes's contributions was his demonstration of the complementarity and interlocking of principles of organization that pulled in different directions: clan alliances, patrilineal kinship, the matrilateral and affinal ties of individuals, and the ritual monopolies of sections of Tallensi communities and their consequent interdependencies with others (1945, 1949b, 1970, 1987). Moreover, his interests in psychology and sociology gave him a double perspective, a preoccupation with the social location and ties of affection of the individual and a larger-scale conception of the social structural framework of groups, particularly corporate ones. When he sought to make an analytic distinction between the domestic domain and the politico-jural domain, he recognized that in practice many of the same social relations belonged to both (1970, 63). Although this jural-domestic distinction did not constitute one of his most felicitous formulations, it sparked considerable discussion of the public/private dichotomy in the setting of African cultural forms. Similarly, his conception of the "axiom of prescriptive altruism" (1970, 251) foreshadowed many subsequent discussions of the way obligatory generosity figures in African thought and social practice.

Fortes, then, can be said to have written in the normative style of the day and to have been intently focused on standardized behavior, on the mandatory and the customary. He peppered this with illustrations, caveats, and exceptions from his fieldwork experience, however. He took very seriously the idea of cultural continuity and noted that the "Tallensi always stress the importance of passing on to their descendants the way of life bequeathed to them by their forefathers" (1945, 25). But in the same breath Fortes hastened to say, "This does not mean that Tale customs never change, or that the Tallensi believe this to be the case, or invariably resist cultural changes. There have been many shifts in custom and usage during the past two decades" (1945, 25). Thus, like many of his contemporaries, he stressed the changes that the colonial administration had brought. He was not unaware of a deeper history, however. So, for example, when he indicated that the Tallensi were closely related to a number of other peoples of the Voltaic region in what are now Ghana and Burkina Faso, he speculated about their historical connections. "The ethnographic picture of to-day suggests that the population of the Voltaic region was, in the past, constantly being redistributed by migrations of small groups" (1945, 7). Fortes also took the time factor into account in the analysis of the shorter term (1949a). He initiated an interest in the developmental cycle of the joint family (1949b, 63) that later led to the important further elaboration of this theme by his student and successor to the Cambridge professorship, Jack Goody (1958).

As in much of Fortes's other work, in his writings on religious thought Fortes was struck by the themes of contradiction and complementarity. In *Oedipus and Job in West African Religion* (1983), he addressed the contrast between the idea of fate—epitomized by the Oedipus story— of a destiny in which individual lives are preordained and individuals are not responsible for their actions, and the opposite idea, epitomized by the biblical story of Job and lived out in the exactions of ancestors among the Tallensi, that not only does individual responsibility exist but that supernatural justice will hold individuals responsible (1983, 3; for an interesting critique, see Jackson 1989, 39–50). Fortes considered the vigilance of the ancestors and their presumed powers over the living to epitomize supernatural justice in the Tallensi milieu. Goody, in an appreciative introduction, wrote that Fortes showed "how ancestor worship and destiny not only operate in Tale social life but also represent, at another level, widespread facets of the human situation" (Fortes 1983, viii). Goody appraises Fortes's contribution as "one of the most important ethnographic achievements of the twentieth century" (ibid., vii).

Fortes's friend and sometime teacher from his South African days, Isaac Schapera, also contributed to this explosion of Africanist ethnography with a pair of monographs on the Tswana of Bechuanaland, *A Handbook of Tswana Law and Custom* (1938) and *Married Life in an African Tribe* (1940; see also Schapera 1928, 1956). Schapera was a skeptical and fact-minded critic in the arena of British anthropology. He had some antipathy for the theoretical ambitions of his colleagues and a strong interest in practical questions, in administration, and in social change during a period when that topic had not yet become the center of theoretical discourse. Schapera's work among the Tswana has been heavily relied upon by all subsequent ethnographers of the area, and his voice was an important one among Africanists for many years as professor at the London School of Economics and successor of Malinowski.

The period was a rich one in African ethnography. Audrey Richards published her *Land, Labour, and Diet in Northern Rhodesia* (1939) on the Bemba. (See also Richards 1955, 1959.) M. Green published *Land Tenure in an Ibo Village* in 1941. (See also Green 1947.) S. F. Nadel wrote *A Black Byzantium* (1942), a remarkably "modern" and complex monograph on the Nupe kingdom as a totality, addressing its political structure, its villages and towns, its economy in the colonial period, and its general history. (See also Nadel 1954.) Nadel later published one of the clearest statements of the theoretical paradigm of the Radcliffe-Brown school, *The Theory of Social Structure* (1967). In 1947 Hilda Kuper published *An African Aristocracy: Rank among the Swazi,* a sketch of an African kingdom's constitutive structure. Like Nadel's work, it addressed a unit much larger and more complex than a village, lineage, or clan. Phyllis Kaberry wrote *Women of the Grassfields* (1952), a pathbreaking study of women in the Bamenda Grassfields, Cameroon. Monica Wilson soon began publishing what were to become a long series of monographs on the Nyakyusa (1952, 1957, 1959, 1977). Aidan Southall proposed a new political paradigm, the "segmentary state," in his analysis of Alur society. He subsequently further developed (1956, 1988) this innovative concept, and it has proved to be analytically durable and useful. These are only some of the products of this very active period of monographic writing, because it defies summary description.

Another major figure to emerge in anthropology in these decades was C. Daryll Forde. His first impact on the field came in 1934 with the publication of his classic comparative work on ecology and culture, *Habitat, Economy, and Society.* He had studied in the United States, where he had come into contact with the culture-area tradition and its ecological orientation. The latter was strongly manifest in his 1934 book. His later fieldwork in southern Nigeria provided unsettling evidence of the great importance of secret societies and other nonkinship-based associations (1956, 1964), complicating the picture of African social organization even at the village level. The heavy emphasis that Radcliffe-Brown, Fortes, and Evans-Pritchard had put on lineage organization clearly represented only one aspect of a much more complex galaxy of variant organizational forms. Anthropology had to enlarge its conceptual tool kit.

Forde had very wide-ranging interests, and he published on everything from African thought to applied anthropology, from African history to colonial government (1939, 1953, 1954, 1967; Forde and Scott 1946; Forde and Kaberry 1967). Forde played a pivotal role in the development of African studies in anthropology. As director of the International African Institute, as editor of *Africa* and also of the *Ethnographic Survey of Africa,* and as professor at University College, London, his importance in furthering the field can scarcely be sufficiently emphasized. Although his was not as strong a voice in the production of theoretical models as were those of Evans-Pritchard and Fortes and the University of London lacked the prestige of Oxbridge, his conception of the breadth of the discipline, his own ethnographic and historical contributions, and his tireless organizational labors to further African studies left an enduring legacy. African studies would never have developed as it did without his remarkable presence.

The work of this whole first generation of post-Malinowskian Africanists falls into two main genres. One was the closed description of the way of life of particular African peoples, a kind of timeless abstraction of "the way it probably was" before the colonial period, as if native life could be conceived as a self-contained system uncontaminated by outside contacts. The second mode of description was entirely different and was concerned with the historical moment at which the fieldwork was done. This genre provided data on everything from labor migration to the impact of colonial institutions. Not only were monographs turned out in the timeless typological mode, but work in the second, contemporary-historical mode was produced virtually from the beginning of the florescence of Africanist fieldwork. Only the first approach fitted into Radcliffe-Brown's comparative project, however, and consequently only the first was treated as theoretically worthy and potentially productive of social laws and theoretical inference. Its artificial timelessness has recently been excoriated as an expression of a colonial, "orientalist" attitude (Fabian 1983).

Although that dimension undoubtedly forms part of the construction of timeless typological ethnography from the perspective of intellectual history, the typologizing legacy of an earlier evolutionism would also seem to have had a substantial part in the making of the structural-functional genre. In addition, it should not be forgotten that many of the same people produced monographs and articles in a very different mode. Thus, not only did Monica Hunter (later Wilson) write *Reaction to Conquest* in 1936, but Fortes wrote "Culture Contact as a Dynamic Process" in 1936, and Max Gluckman wrote "Analysis of a Social Situation in Modern Zululand" (1940), on the ceremony marking the opening of a bridge in which colonial officials and Zulus participated, as well as *The Economy of the Central Barotse Plain* (1941), in which he noted the effect of World War II on Barotseland (see also Gluckman 1942, 1943a, 1943b,

1949). Godfrey Wilson wrote *An Essay on the Economics of De-tribalization in Northern Rhodesia* in 1942. Schapera published *Migrant Labor and Tribal Life* in 1947 (see also Read 1938; Firth 1947; Forde 1937, 1939; Forde and Scott 1946; Bohannan 1954, 1955, 1959; Richards, 1939, 1955; Gulliver 1955a, 1955b, 1958; Smith 1955).

To ignore the time-conscious implications of these writings in order better to attack the static models of Radcliffe-Brownian structural-functionalism is certainly a legitimate polemic strategy, but such arguments tend to mispresent the most interesting peculiarities of the discipline at the time. In keeping with the conception of social change described by the Wilsons in 1945, British anthropologists' discussion of Africa in the 1930s, 1940s, and into the 1950s presumed both the validity of their reconstructions of "traditional systems" and the reality of a very different, observed contemporary situation. A grand theoretical overvalorization of the "traditional" and the "tribal" limited their capacity to see the artificiality of their retrospective constructions, and more significantly it gave a peculiar twist to their conceptions of change. They not only thought that "modern" Africa was less interesting theoretically than "traditional" Africa, but they also did not like it as much. It seemed to them less African, less what had attracted them to African studies in the first place. The scholars were well aware of a living Africa that was not the "traditional" one of the comparative models, however, and many of them also wrote about that living Africa.

This was to become more and more the case, and a great push in that direction was given by the research done at the Rhodes-Livingstone Institute in Northern Rhodesia. Its first director was Godfrey Wilson, who was preoccupied with a changing Africa. He thought that research should be undertaken among urban Africans and in the townships of the mining areas, not only in the rural countryside. When violent strikes broke out in 1940, Wilson was obliged to end his research in the Broken Hill mining township because the colonial authorities withdrew permission for him to continue. "By so-called fraternisation with the subject group, the anthropologist aroused the resentment of the dominant Europeans who saw their norms being flouted by men who . . . were in any case distrusted" (Brown 1973, 193). In the midst of these difficulties, Wilson resigned as director in 1941.

Max Gluckman, who had joined the institute in 1939 and had started fieldwork on the Lozi kingdom in rural Barotseland then succeeded him as director. Although Gluckman implemented many of Wilson's plans for research, he went far beyond them, because he had his own view of the transformations occurring in British Central Africa. Gluckman was much less of a Malinowskian than Wilson, not at all convinced that the breaking up of a tribal way of life was the central issue in the study of change. His interest in conflict was crucial to this difference of perspective. The outcome of conflict, as he saw it, was sociologically most interesting when it produced one of two results— when the end of a dispute reaffirmed previous social relationships and cultural norms or when it produced radical change. He interpreted the resolution of disputes between individuals largely as norm affirming but saw political conflict and group conflict as potentially transformative and revolutionary. Gluckman saw African society as inherently conservative. Although one chief might rebel against and assassinate another or one ruling lineage might replace another, once in office the new incumbent would tend to perpetuate the political structure. Gluckman distinguished between rebellion and revolution in this way: rebellion merely produced a replacement of personnel in key positions of power, but revolution actually altered the political economy. Gluckman considered himself something of a Marxist, hence the analytic emphasis on revolution (see Moore 1978). This polar model of change suited a structural-functional vision of precolonial African political systems and also accounted for the durability of the native-colonial relationship. Gluckman clearly held a radically subversive view of the colonial situation but a rather static conception of precolonial African society.

However neat this model of a polar opposition between

structural continuity and structural replacement, the framework did not accommodate incremental change and made it difficult to address the common experience that continuity and change can be simultaneous and intertwined dynamic processes in a society. Later in his life, Gluckman tried to repair this theoretical gap in his concept of process. In response to the challenges of Fredrik Barth and the general rejection of Radcliffe-Brownian theory that took place in the 1960s, Gluckman constructed and elaborated on the notion of a "moving equilibrium." But the theoretical framework that appears in much of his earlier writing was the oppositional one. Werbner (1984) has represented Gluckman's perspective as "a dialectical view" and, in part, it was (163). Gluckman did not make his most remarkable contributions to anthropological thought as a theorist of change. Rather, he did so as a dogged and insistent investigator of conflict and competition in many settings; by methodologically using the "case method" in ethnography; by approaching African law in a manner that went beyond the "rules and norms" style of his predecessors to study litigation; by insisting on the legitimacy of doing unconventional, nontribal ethnography in modern Africa; and as an organizer, encourager, goad, and critic of the research of others. (See Gluckman 1940, 1941, 1942, 1949, 1955, 1965, 1975.)

What Malinowski and later Radcliffe-Brown provided to a whole generation of Africanists in England, Gluckman represented at the Rhodes-Livingstone Institute in Africa and later at Manchester. He had the added advantage of having grown up in South Africa and being passionately aware of the kind of political economy many Africans lived in, as laborers in the mines and dwellers in the townships. He incorporated the structural-functional vision in some of his work on rural, "tribal" Africa, but he also broke with that conception both theoretically and methodologically and encouraged others to do so, as he and the people with whom he surrounded himself at the Rhodes-Livingstone Institute broke new ground. Gluckman devised a seven-year research plan for the institute that was addressed to studying "British Central Africa as a changing society" with a heavy emphasis on the changing economy of both rural and urban areas (Werbner 1984, 163).

The institute was financed by colonial governments and by the copper companies, but it remained "a surprisingly independent centre of learning" and was "the servant of neither" the colonial authorities nor the copper companies (Brown 1973, 197). Under Gluckman's direction and under its subsequent leaders, Elizabeth Colson and Clyde Mitchell, the Rhodes-Livingstone Institute served as a locus of enormous anthropological productivity. It funded fieldwork. Colson's remarkable series of articles and monographs on the Tonga, which started in a classical British social anthropological mode of reconstruction and gradually diverged into contemporary commentary, are striking examples of the kind of work associated with the institute, as is Mitchell's book on the Yao together with his subsequent innovative excursions into urban work and network analysis (see Colson 1948, 1953, 1958, 1960b, 1962, 1971; Colson and Gluckman 1951; Colson and Scudder 1975; Mitchell 1956, 1966, 1968, 1969). As important as its sponsorship of fieldwork was the institute's role as a center for the presentation of work in progress and for a critical discussion of the issues involved.

Just as the LSE and later the Oxford school had been a nucleus for the development of new ideas when the number of Africanists involved formed a critical mass with common interests that gave the analytic enterprise tremendous impetus, so did the Rhodes-Livingstone Institute become a hothouse for new subject matter, new research methods, and new theoretical constructs. The connection with anthropologists in Britain remained close, and later, after 1949, when Gluckman migrated to Manchester University to head the department there, many of the people who had been with him in central Africa also spent time at Manchester. The theoretical wave that had begun at Rhodes-Livingstone became a tide. The Manchester school came to have an identity of its own, but the influence of the new approaches spread far beyond northern England.

Not only was a great deal of new research done under the auspices of the Rhodes-Livingstone Institute, but two approaches relatively new to social anthropology became built into the fieldwork enterprise— the collection of statistical data and the collection of extended case histories (see Epstein 1967a). The statistical data were collected not only to have a more precise knowledge of what was going on in the Central African setting but also to make possible systematic comparisons between societies. On the other hand, microsocial research, studying the activities of particular individuals in particular situations, often in conflict and competition, made new inferences possible about the choices and pressures under which individuals acted. Thus, Gluckman's famous paper (1940) on the dedication of a bridge in Zululand was a description of a nontraditional ritual, a coming together on a ceremonial occasion of Europeans and Zulus who had very different interests and attitudes both to the moment and to one another. The strategizing of individuals and their subjection to hierarchies of power showed both how the system worked and how individuals worked the system. In another paper, Gluckman showed how in the colonial situation village headmen were caught between the pressures of their kinsmen and neighbors and the pressures exerted by persons higher in the official bureaucratic system (Gluckman 1949).

But at the same time that he took these strides forward into new analytical territory, Gluckman remained within the long-established mode in a great deal of his work, looking for the traditional in the Barotse world, reconstructing the culture in terms of stated ideal norms instead of collecting extensive data on actual practices. As he remarked when asked why he had not carried further forward in his own fieldwork the kind of situational interest that he showed in the ceremony at the bridge, he replied, "Perhaps this was because it was ahead of its time, and I belonged after all of my own generation" (Epstein 1967a, xx). But the Rhodes-Livingstone group and the Manchester University department used the two new approaches extensively, even though their leader had not done much of this in his own ethnographic work. (See in particular the work of Kapferer [1972, 1976] and that of Mitchell [1966, 1969].) Intellectually,

Gluckman was characterized by complex and creative inconsistencies, all forcefully stated. He recognized a good idea when he saw one and gave great, although sometimes rather argumentative, encouragement to those with whom he worked. His colleagues at Rhodes-Livingstone had his full attention even when they did not have his full agreement. At Manchester he was a strong presence and established the character of the department. It was no accident that the critique of a normative anthropology animated many of his colleagues.

Much as Gluckman encouraged the microsociological accounts produced by some of his colleagues, he also saw the great value of expanding field data statistically to a larger scale when feasible. His interest in social problems and his plan for the Rhodes-Livingstone Institute involved a wide spectrum of modes of study. It was evident from the start that urban areas could not be studied effectively in what had been the conventional Oxford way of addressing rural society, in the mold of total "tribal systems" with a focus on kinship organization. Moreover, in central Africa, the "total system" had to include the colonial presence, industrial enterprise, and migrant labor. At the Rhodes-Livingstone Institute the assembling of fine-grained case studies was as characteristic of the work as was the use of sociological techniques of sampling and surveying and the study of social networks. (See Epstein 1967a as well as Werbner 1984.) As Gluckman said in his introduction to Epstein's *The Craft of Social Anthropology* (1967a), "The contributors are anthropologists who have had the opportunity of working closely together for many years either as officers of the Rhodes-Livingstone Institute, or in the Department of Social Anthropology at Manchester University, or both. . . . My colleagues . . . have developed research techniques far beyond those I myself employed when I was last in the field." Gluckman went on to point out that there are essentially two techniques represented in the essays, "the consistent attempt to quantify variables as far as possible . . . [and] the concentration on detailed analysis of social situations and extended cases" (xii).

Despite what now seems his rather old-fashioned personal

ethnographic agenda in the Barotse work, to reconstruct as best he could a no-longer-existing "tribal political system," Gluckman's fieldwork among the Lozi nevertheless broke new ground. He was the first ethnographer to spend substantial time listening to legal cases in an African court. When he wrote up this material, he not only described the procedure of the hearings, the facts of the cases, and their outcomes, but he also attempted to generalize about the mode of reasoning used by the African judges and to explain the Lozi normative system as they saw it (Gluckman 1955). Although various shortcomings of this work are now apparent, perhaps most glaringly its ahistoricity, its method alone represented a pathbreaking achievement at the time, and it has stimulated much further research in law and anthropology, a field to which Gluckman's contribution gave a new form. In many earlier ethnographies African law was routinely given a chapter or two, but in those chapters law was conventionally described as a set of "tribal" constitutional principles and list of norms. Gluckman consciously sought to obtain more detailed knowledge of a "primitive" legal system along the lines of Sir Henry Maines's model (see Moore 1978). In fact, as it turned out, both Gluckman's method and his observations led him in unexpected directions. He was intellectually open enough to follow what he saw rather than to see what he had expected. Once again, the African evidence altered the course of theory-building. The idea of observing an African people in the midst of their disputations and litigations as one might in a Western court was an entirely new one. This was the case method in one of its early incarnations. There were others to come.

Victor Turner's *Schism and Continuity in an African Society: A Study of Ndembu Village Life* (1957) is an example of the way members of the Rhodes-Livingstone and Manchester groups not only used but went considerably beyond the problematic set by Gluckman and built new wings on the house of the Oxbridge social structuralists. First of all, like many of the Rhodes-Livingstone products, Turner's book was about village life, not about "the tribe" writ large. Second, the work concerned itself with structure not as an integrated harmonious whole, as Radcliffe-Brown might have conceived it, but as an entity thoroughly riddled with conflict. Strains were built into its very normative core. Third, Turner's research methods included an innovative use of a detailed extended case about particular persons in a particularly drawn-out dispute about the succession to a headmanship. Turner called his long case histories "social dramas," and he presented disputes over succession and inheritance and their management as ultimately group-affirming. He made a similar interpretation of the use of ritual in situations of conflict (1967, 1968, 1975). But despite this Gluckmanesque commitment to the paradox that group cohesion can be an important social product of conflict, the technique by which he demonstrated this theory was much more than a normative structural-functional statement about groups. It concerned struggles and confrontations and the process of group maintenance under divisive circumstances. Turner's "social drama" described the way things came about over a particular period of time. His account was temporally situated and quite specifically so.

Of the conflicts that interested Turner, one was central to Ndembu life— the fact that although a village was supposed to be grouped around a core of matrilineally related men the same men who wanted a sister's son in the village also tried to keep their own adult sons and the mothers of these sons with them. In the presence of these dual pulls, the contradictory attractions of matrilineality and virilocality, the composition of villages was inherently unstable, and marriages were also unstable. And although Turner generalized in classical normative terms about Ndembu rules of residence and marriage and the like, he also enlarged this information with statistical surveys of a number of villages in which he showed the incidence of conformity and nonconformity. These surveys were temporally and geographically situated— they were made in a particular year about particular places and persons. Through these practices, although it was not consciously rejected, the ahistorical normative structural-functional mold was in fact broken.

The emphasis on competition and conflict, on the specific extended case history and on the statistical survey were to become hallmarks of Rhodes-Livingstone research and of what subsequently came to be known as the Manchester school. The temporal and situational specificity of the data collected and the fact that it involved real individuals, not just an account of "traditions," marked an emerging change of ethnographic technique that had profound theoretical consequences.

Migration and Urban Life: Transformable Identities

In the African situation, whenever analytic attention was focused on rural-urban relations or on the movement of persons from one domain to the other (or to other labor centers, such as plantations and mines), it was obvious that the "tribes" from which those people came could no longer be imagined as closed autonomous entities. The African countryside clearly was imbedded in a much larger set of political and economic relations, as was made plain by rural contact with the agents and agencies of the colonial administration, with missionaries and with settlers, with cash cropping and tax paying, let alone the membership of Africans in a migratory labor force. The rural areas fed the towns and cities and supplied them (and the plantations and mines) with labor. In turn, the cities ruled the countryside, taxed it, and regulated it.

The changes wrought by these circumstances began to be prominent in the writings of anthropologists from the late 1930s on and came into their own in the subsequent decades. Very early on, these works, unlike "tribal" studies, focused on the changes wrought by the colonial presence. (See, for example, Hunter 1936; Mair 1938; Richards 1939, 1940; Wilson 1968.) Colonial administrations not only had a strong political interest in the attitudes of town-dwelling Africans but also worried about the effects labor migration might have on the rural countryside. (See Gulliver 1955b; Read 1942; Schapera 1947.) Political involvement in migration issues has, of course, continued in the postcolonial period. And no wonder, because

African cities and towns have continued to grow at an increasingly rapid rate. Thus, it follows that there has been an ongoing and connected anthropological interest in the causes and consequences of migration and there have been a number of efforts to produce generalizable models of the variables involved (see, for example Parkin 1975).

At midcentury, when many African rural communities were already substantially involved in the migrant labor stream, many villages found that the migrants' cash added to their resources without introducing new and serious problems. Others were less appropriately organized and suffered profound disruptions of their internal economies because of the absence of the migrants. The Mambwe of Northern Rhodesia were among the more fortunate peoples. Through a variety of strategies of patrilineal cooperation, they managed to avoid the potential ill effects on their agriculture of the absence of their young men (Watson 1958). Less cooperatively structured communities were much harder hit: Audrey Richards (1939) demonstrated that in some Bemba villages all the young men were absent at one time, with disastrous effects, while in others all the men remained, and agriculture proceeded normally. Gluckman's fieldwork on Barotse court cases collected in the 1940s showed a predominance of family conflicts. The cases often alluded to the absence of male family members as the source of these domestic problems (see Gluckman 1955). The reorganization of African life was felt in many domains (Forde 1956b; Gluckman 1961; Wilson 1968).

In a more recent period, new crises have again shifted the subject. Attention to the relations between town and countryside have not only focused on the flow of population to the towns but on the food supply for cities. Anthropologists have joined an important and growing interdisciplinary conversation about the consequences of political and economic policies bearing on these questions. The connections among culture, history, politics, and economy in Africa are nowhere more visible than in the study of urban food supplies. (For persuasive interdisciplinary demonstrations, see Guyer 1987; Bates 1981;

and Morrison and Gutkind 1982.) From the point of view of the history of the discipline, the links between town and country have at several junctures played a crucial part in the opening up of anthropology to untraditional and larger-than-local issues, practical and theoretical.

It is probably no accident that several of the earliest descriptions by anthropologists of town life and of labor migration should have been generated in South Africa, where all of these phenomena were firmly established sooner than they were in many other parts of the continent (see Hellmann 1935, 1937, 1948, 1949; Schapera 1947). Attention to these nonexotic topics obliged anthropologists to construct new ways of going about their business. Neither ethnography nor analysis could proceed as they had before. (For some useful bibliographies, books, and articles on African labor migration and on African cities by or including work by anthropologists, see Balandier 1955; Diop 1965; Meillassoux 1968; Gugler and Flanagan 1978; Gulliver 1955b; Mitchell 1956, 1966, 1968, 1969, 1987; Epstein 1958, 1967a, 1967b, 1978; Forde 1956b; Southall 1961, 1973; Parkin 1969, 1975, 1978; Kapferer 1972; Lloyd 1966, 1974; Lloyd, Mabogunje, and Awe 1967; Kuper 1965; Little 1970, 1973; Gutkind 1974; Gutkind and Wallerstein 1985; MacGaffey 1987; Miner 1967; Morrison and Gutkind 1982; Southall and Gutkind 1956.)

Portable Knowledge and Mutable Connections

The concept of the "tribe" as the model of African life had many features that could not easily be transposed to the analysis of urban settings. For one thing, the "tribal" was thought of as "tradition" incarnate, as the very picture of an enduring cultural system reenacted from generation to generation (Southall 1970). The town was, of course, the opposite— the place of change, new friends, new habits, new ideas.

Classical conceptions of the "tribe" located culture and social relationships together in the same theoretical space, totally intertwined and mutually reinforcing and validating. Cultural forms were seen as metaphoric "representations" of customary kinship and village social relations. In this idea of "tribal" society, culture served as a prescribed, reiterative medium of social communication that repeatedly represented the social order and reenacted it in symbolic form.

Yet once migrants had left for town it was likely that such cultural reenactments would cease to have as large a place in their daily affairs, if any. They left behind the rural arena of social life that had been infused with a single local cultural style. For migrant workers in town the previously continuous experience of a native cultural world was reduced to being a memory, a form of knowledge the migrants carried in their heads. "Tribal" cultural knowledge was separated from its normal social milieu.

Anthropologists working in towns had to construct a new way of interpreting the significance of that portable knowledge of a "culture" once the cultural ideas and habits had become disconnected from the original social environment. In town the migrant's culture had lost its anthropologically postulated "tribal social functions." Three kinds of questions needed to be answered. One was the ethnographic question of how the migrants' consciousness of their own "tribal" origin affected their new lives. A second was the theoretical question of what sort of an urban model could be constructed to accommodate the realities of African towns. And third, what effect did the departure and return of migrants have, both on the village and on the anthropologists' theory of the insulated "tribal" village?

"Tribes" had been treated as total social systems, controlling their inhabitants. The members of "tribal" groups were conceived as persons conforming to a pervasive normative culture that prescribed their "status"— i.e., their social positions in the system— and specified their "roles." Anthropologists working within that paradigm sought to discover the integrating logic that held the whole culture together and drove the continued reproduction of the social structure. Thus, "tribal" interpretation focused on "custom."

The cities and towns were not predominantly the locus of

custom. Nothing was more apparent than that social reproduction was not the order of the day. Evidence of ongoing change existed everywhere. Continuous improvisation and innovation took place as new waves of Africans moved in, found work, made their way into the cash economy, and generated new relationships, new ideas, new tastes, and new forms of recreation. They were living in a culturally plural setting. Some means had to be devised of analyzing that milieu and of addressing change and its results. Whatever that was, it had to be as theoretically persuasive as the still-dominant functional study of "tribal" custom.

From "Tribe" to Town: Shifts of Scope and Method

First of all, there was the problem of how much of the town to study or, rather, what part of it to study and how to do that. In rural areas, the scope of the universe that could be intensively observed by an anthropologist was usually defined by mechanical constraints. The groups of persons and the geographical area that could be studied was normally small. The practical imperatives of the fieldwork situation dictated the physical limits of intensive observation. In the countryside, anthropologists used a theoretical tour de force to turn that necessity into a virtue. Local units, kin groups, hamlets, and villages came to be thought of as the prototypical building blocks of which the "larger society" was composed. The organization of the local community was abstracted. Its analytically distilled "structure" could then be treated as an exemplar of many identical organizations. A high level of structural replication was presumed to be typical of "tribal" society.

If each sub-unit contained in its form and practice the blueprint of a basic structure, what connected it to other like units? Standardized social relationships— i.e., the conventional social links within, between, and among local units— were regarded as the social adhesive that shaped and held the "whole" together. Kinship, religion, ritual, economic production, exchange, leadership, and warfare all were remarked on "structurally"— that is, in their "functions" as social dividers or connectors, definers of relationships. Apart from important differences associated with gender and age and in some cases dependent on rank, everyone was presumed to participate in all of these domains in very similar ways.

Why, in the British school, did the analysis of "tribes" so emphasize social relations? The answer may lie partly in the policy of indirect rule, which by definition used local social systems for its implementation. Converging with this practical need was an intellectual reaction to aspects of the Durkheimian theory of the primitive. If the division of labor was the adhesive that held industrial societies together, as Durkheim thought, what made "primitive" societies cohere? Durkheim postulated that the primitive societal adhesive was cultural homogeneity (1966).

This Durkheimian vision was a conception of two entirely different bases of cohesion for industrial and tribal societies. It defined tribal society as lacking what industrial society had, i.e., complementary social relationships founded on occupational specialization. To undo the mistakes of fact in that oversimple comparison, redefining the tribal became an essential part of the structural-functional anthropological project. Anthropologists sought to show in ethnographic detail the actual extensive, cohesion-producing social relations of "tribes," the relations of exchange that constituted the functional equivalent of those produced by the division of labor.

The emphasis on examining the nature of individual and collective social relationships could be transferred effectively to the study of people in towns, but in other respects many of the lessons of the "tribal" model were useless. Few towns were culturally homogeneous (Mitchell 1960, 1966, 1969; Smith and Kuper 1969). Many towns included people from different ethnic groups and usually also people from a variety of classes and nationalities. Towns epitomized the division of labor. By definition they usually included numerous specialized governmental, religious, educational, and commercial organizations. Towns formed part of the composite social "whole" of the colonial state.

Unless anthropologists shifted from participant observation to survey research (and some did) they could not address the town as a whole. Fieldwork, the classical anthropological method, had to consciously focus on specialized subsegments of these complex, diverse settlements. An awareness that in town one was studying parts of societies and juxtaposed cultures rather than a single set of putatively unitary "tribal" customs was an important feature in the urban anthropologist's consciousness. Once selected, the fieldwork site stood in the foreground, but behind it was a vast background that included the rest of the urban area with its likely population of colonial officials, managers of enterprises, missionaries, schoolteachers, shopkeepers, and the like. Behind that at a somewhat greater distance were the rural areas from which the African population came.

In town, there had to be a theoretical and/or practical logic to drawing the boundary of the ethnographic problem at a particular point, and techniques had to be devised for sketching in the larger context. The emphasis on the fact that only a part, not the "whole society," was studied represented a major departure from monographs in the "tribal" mode. The study of a part, a piece, an instance, a theme has now become a standard approach in anthropology, when virtually all milieu are seen as parts of larger "complexes," usually heterogeneous, and in the midst of transformation. This recasting of the ethnographic problematic appeared in one of its earliest anthropological forms in studies of African migration and urbanization.

With such a creative agenda, the study of Africans in urban environments inevitably generated profound differences among anthropologists about what questions to ask and how to understand events. For the new problems, no "dominant paradigm" existed. Balandier, who was very familiar with the work of the Rhodes-Livingstone group, relied on sampling in sociological surveys (1955). In the British school, several general approaches competed. Although important, those differences of conception have been overlooked in recent writings. They express deep-running political attitudes and reveal aspects of the ideological climate in which anthropologists worked during the colonial period. Some of the ways of thinking about Africans and African urban affairs established in that period have proved to have a very long life.

From early on in the urban work, one can distinguish three definitions of the research problem that recur at different levels of intensity, sometimes in a blended form. The first definition addresses the character of "an African city" studied as a totality. In this approach there was an implied (or less often an explicit) comparison with other cities of the world. The second definition asks the question of how much of the rural "tribal" system African migrants imported into town: How "tribal" did they remain? Or, to the same effect but from a different point of departure, how many African "tribal" values and ideas were eroded, lost, or replaced as they encountered colonial ideas and institutions? The third approach saw urban Africans primarily as workers in a colonial economy. The questions raised in this approach tended to concentrate on what the Africans experienced and did as laborers. The place of tribal origin was a matter of interest only as the workers themselves made something of it in their new lives.

The early urban studies were inevitably informed by existing sociological conceptions of "the city" and a conventional set of typologies generated in a European context about the way the urban differed from the rural. Weber, Marx, and Durkheim were well known in anthropology, as was the work of the Chicago school of sociologists. A model of "the modern" or "civilized" city matched the paradigm of the "tribal" or "folk" society of rural areas (see, for example, Weber 1962; Wirth 1938; Redfield 1941; and Wilson and Wilson 1968). Comparisons among social types were imbued with evolutionary assumptions. In the discourse of the time, the stages of evolution toward modernity were assumed to be exemplified by different types of cities, i.e., those with stronger urban characteristics and those showing fewer, weaker levels of "urbanism." This model was applied to Africa by Horace Miner, one of Redfield's students.

The City as a Totality

In 1940, Horace Miner went to Timbuctoo specifically to study what he assumed was a pure example of African urbanism that predated the colonial period and hence had not been deeply formed (or radically restructured) by contact with the Euro-American tradition. He intended to test the cross-cultural applicability of Redfield's evolutionary idea that urban development could be studied as a matter of degree. Redfield assumed that the transition from rural to urban was best conceived as a continuum. Given that understanding, he believed that surviving exemplars of the various stages of urban development could be studied in the field. He had, in fact, done so himself by comparing three communities in Yucatan. Miner tried to apply something of the model to Timbuctoo, but he radically altered the method. Miner did not compare communities but looked at one city and tried to measure how "urban" it was. In an effort to do this quantitatively, he ran into serious problems. He used a definitional list of the characteristics of "a city" as if they could be turned into a set of measurable qualities, and he taxed Redfield for the generality and imprecision of the list (Miner 1953, 268). Miner had no doubt that "commerce . . . was the activity that drew the heterogeneous population of Timbuctoo together" and that impersonal relations motivated by profit-seeking characterized the interethnic market (ibid., 272–73).

Later monographs on "cities as wholes" did not confront the Miner-Redfield degree-of-urbanism problem but tended to examine the characteristics of particular towns without trying to fit them into a single comparative scale. The implicit assumption was that towns differed one from another in so many qualities that it would be reductive and therefore distorting to try to place them on a single continuum. The particularities were worth studying as such. In these later works that examined towns as totalities, they tended to be treated descriptively, noting their multiple dimensions as physical spaces in which political, social, and economic activities were organized and carried on (Banton 1957; Epstein 1958; Hopkins 1972; Lloyd, Mabogunje, and Awe 1967; Southall and Gutkind 1956). Persons and goods flowed in and out. The towns had important relations with rural areas and with other urban centers. These sketches of towns as "wholes" inevitably tended to be sociological and quantitative in style.

The enormous difference between the old towns and cities of West Africa, whose history went deep into the past, and the relatively new towns and cities of East Africa, established by colonial governments as administrative and industrial centers, evoked frequent comment (Epstein 1967b; Gutkind 1974; Kuper 1965; Southall 1961). This difference has importance not only historically but analytically, because some of the older towns and cities are more ethnically homogeneous or more clearly dominated by a particular ethnic group, whereas the newer centers have generally been culturally plural from the start.

The history and social structure of African towns and cities, let alone of concentrations of population at plantations and mines, were and are exceedingly varied. The details of that variation have considerable importance for understanding the economy and politics of postcolonial Africa, let alone its past.

The Wilsons and the Mayers: The "Detribalization" and "Conservatism" Question

The preoccupation of some scholars with the degree of continued "tribalism" and with the extent of its dismantling in urban Africa had strong, built-in biases. It conceived of Africans as emerging from stable social systems into a state of confusion and disruption, neither fully African nor fully Europeanized. The absence of full "Europeanness" has been remarked on in many forms, usually as an unachievable prize. For example, Balandier (1955) reported sadly that although African children learned French in school, the vocabulary they acquired was understood by means of dictionary definitions. Consequently, they could never achieve full mastery of the "thickness of meaning" of the French language. Teachers reported "une véritable maladie du dictionnaire," and Balandier mused on whether the French and Africans really understood one another when they spoke to each other in French (237).

In the British version of what was happening in this "neither fully African nor fully European" circumstance, African culture was thought of as "breaking down" (see Wilson and Wilson 1968), in a process called "detribalization." That term came to have other political meanings in the postcolonial period, when it became the watchword of certain nationalist movements. In the late colonial period, however, it signified a loss of traditional norms and values, of the old order. In this mode, there was a tendency to romanticize the past, to think of the traditional as having been a fine, highly moral, workable system, its loss a serious deprivation especially in the norms and values department. The Wilsons thought that a new immorality had set in when the tribal order was cast off and that European values had "not yet" been adopted. The implication that they eventually would be (and should be) was clear.

Godfrey and Monica Wilson's *The Analysis of Social Change* ([1945] 1968) was surely the most ambitious (but theoretically conservative) attempt to reconcile the Malinowskian functional model with the study of social transformation in Africa. This book had considerable importance in the history of the discipline, not only because it was very respectfully received by British Africanist anthropologists at the time, but also because it revealed a vision of change as "instability" that was probably widely shared during the late colonial period. Part of its emotional background was undoubtedly the set of conflicts that developed between Europeans and Africans in the mines of the copper belt in what was then Northern Rhodesia. When African miners went on strike in 1935 and six miners were killed by the police in the riots that ensued, it was not possible to think of the situation as benign. The vision of social transformation in the Wilsons' book on social change is understandably gloomy. (See also Wilson 1968.)

Precisely because the theoretical framework of the Wilsons' joint essay, the two "total systems" approach, is unacceptable now, their work gives unparalleled insight into the vagaries of the imagination at that time. The book shows how they could rationalize the fact of change and the theory of functionalism as consistent with each other and also incorporate a strong residue of evolutionism in the bargain. The Wilsons contended that there were basically two kinds of society, the primitive and the civilized, each of them a functionally coherent whole. Each type of society was in equilibrium in its pure form. Once in contact with civilization, however, the primitive balances became destabilized and the pristine functioning totality of indigenous social life came apart. "All objective analysis of social relations rests on the assumption that they form coherent systems, that within any one field they support and determine one another inexorably. The oppositions and maladjustments we have just catalogued, however, show us a field in which social relations are largely incoherent, pulling against and contradicting one another" (Wilson and Wilson 1968, 23).

As the Wilsons saw it, uneven change caused the disruption of African societies because they were partly composed of indigenous institutions and values and partly of borrowed ones. This disruption could be prevented only if the pace of change could be controlled so that all institutions changed equally rapidly (or equally slowly) in tandem (ibid., 168). The Wilsons pleaded for better conditions for Africans. They attacked racism in all its forms. They framed detailed arguments "scientifically" within the thesis that all of central Africa's troubles resulted from societal imbalances consequent from uneven change. If these were corrected, functional equilibrium and cultural coherence could be attained. In this framework, anthropology could hold its own theoretical balance by clinging to a harmonious functional model. This was a vision of two total systems, primitive and civilized, each in a happy equilibrium in its "pure" state.

Trouble arose only in the irregular transition from one to the other.

The pressures of European dominance and the forms of African resistance were nowhere more evident than in urban settings and other centers where African labor was concentrated. Anthropologists, whatever their theoretical positions, were acutely conscious of the violence that erupted intermittently. Greater or lesser attachment to "native culture" was far from the major issue in the lives of African laborers in European enterprises. "Twice in five years Africans have rioted on the Northern Rhodesian copperbelt and have been fired on by the military," wrote Godfrey and Monica Wilson (1968, 14). In their monograph on town-dwelling Xhosa in East London, Cape Province, South Africa, Philip and Iona Mayer said, "The riots of 1952 . . . arose out of what was originally a non-violent protest . . . organized by the African National Congress. . . . The East London authorities forbade all public meetings in the locations. This ban was defied. . . . In breaking up this meeting police used firearms, and several Xhosa (numbers unknown) were accidentally killed or wounded. Violence now broke out," and whites were killed and buildings belonging to whites were attacked and burned (1971, 82). It is interesting that in the Mayers' text the deaths from police action are characterized as accidental and the term *violence* is reserved for what the Africans did in their subsequent rage.

The Mayers were writing many years after the Wilsons, but they remained preoccupied with an enduring question about "tribal" survivals. Among the Xhosa with whom the Mayers worked in East London marked divisions existed between what were called the "school" Xhosa, who were more involved with European institutions (religious, educational, and so forth), and those who aggressively maintained a tribal style in town, the "conservative" or red Xhosa. These school/red distinctions existed in the rural population and predated the migration to town. A shift from one category to the other after settling in East London was socially and culturally difficult. The Mayers put it this way: "Red people 'do not want to get mixed up' in things that tend to obscure the distinction between a 'real Xhosa' and a foreigner. School people are, in some respects, quite glad to do so" (ibid., 41). This statement not only reports two ideological positions of Africans as the Mayers understood them but inadvertently reveals the kind of model the Mayers were using. Their vision of the tribal life was that in tribal areas norms were prescribed and statuses ascribed; in the modern system— i.e., in the town— individuals faced an enormous range of choices from which they could make their own selections. The Mayers allude to and use Firth's distinction between structure and organization to distinguish the two social systems, the rural and the urban. In doing so, however, they rather cavalierly reinterpret Firth, because he had, in fact, used the terms to describe two analytic aspects of the same system (1951). The Mayers conclude their study of African townspeoples "personal, spare time activities" by reiterating this model of tribal constraint and urban choice. "The contrast between migrants' town opportunities and their country opportunities has seemed to be a contrast between the optional and the inescapable, the alternative and the given; the over-all contrast is between organization on the one hand, and structure on the other" (Mayer and Mayer 1971, 284).

The Mayers virtually attribute the difference between school and red Xhosa in town to a matter of personal choice, and, no doubt, the Mayers are correct that the red Xhosa themselves spoke of preferring their own way of life. But, in fact, the model of urban choice does not fit very well with the rich ethnographic data in the Mayers' book, which shows the opposite. Their ethnographic evidence shows that stringent legal, political, and economic determinants constrained the lives of all the South Africans of East London. The same determinants privileged the more Europeanized Africans and permitted some of them a small range of particularly urban cultural choices but made the red Xhosa all the more dependent on keeping their rural ties alive and on maintaining rural cultural practices in the town. The Mayers argue strongly that the red Xhosa lived in town but were not "urbanized," but the Mayers do not consider that this "theoretical" result is simply the product of their limited definition of the urban, their equation of "urban" with detribalized and Europeanized.

Urban Africans as Workers

There was an entirely different way of looking at the matter. The more radical, more politically minded group of anthropologists at the Rhodes-Livingstone Institute rejected the negative, culture-loss perspective out of hand. They saw urban Africans as workers drawn into the world economy. Gluckman and Mitchell were the early pioneers of this school. They saw the town as having many positive aspects, as a new situation in which Africans generated new relationships and forged new cultural ideas in addition to those that were already familiar to them. They were not simply losing their bearings. They were acquiring new skills, new knowledge, and access to a larger world.

William Watson, who studied with Gluckman, argued that "the concept of 'detribalization' implies that an African must choose between two systems of social relations and values, one based on modern industrial production, the other on traditional subsistence production: if he is absorbed into industry this necessarily dissolves his tribal social relations and the moral values implicit in them. But a man can participate in two different spheres of social relations and keep them distinct and separate. . . . The two economic and social spheres [rural and urban] are spatially and socially distinct, and although men undoubtedly carry ideas from one to the other, the spheres exist conjointly" (1958, 6).

Watson's fieldwork among the rural Mambwe of what was then Northern Rhodesia is an interesting demonstration of just that thesis, because all Mambwe men entered the migrant labor stream for certain periods of time between the ages of eighteen and forty-five but returned intermittently to their villages and eventually resettled there permanently (ibid., 70). Young men most urgently wanted to earn money for marriage payments.

The Later Colonial Period

Later they wanted cash with which to buy the European goods they considered necessary for the new material way of life that had come to the village. As Max Gluckman pointed out in his introduction to Watson's book, however, "The basis of the continuing tribal system is the land; and land is the ultimate security for the Mambwe in so far as they participate in the modern economy" (ibid., xi). African migrant laborers did not necessarily give up their right to resume a villager's political place as well as their right to claim a piece of village land. But these latent rural rights were not directly relevant to the way of life in the town.

Gluckman distanced himself from the conception that "tribalism" was a single sociological phenomenon, a set of ideas that Africans carried with them from the country to the city in some sort of mental package. Alluding to the innovative urban work of Clyde Mitchell and A. L. Epstein, Gluckman said, "They have shown that tribalism in urban areas is something quite different from tribalism in the rural areas: in urban areas, tribal ties link people in many forms of association, but are not an organized system of relations involved in the bases of production or in political authority" (introduction to Watson 1958, xi). In town, the place of tribal origin was the basis of newly formed urban ethnic associations, but in the countryside tribal membership was the foundation of political and economic citizenship.

A pivotal publication that reveals the attitude of the post-Wilson Rhodes-Livingstone group toward the ethnic issue was Clyde Mitchell's *The Kalela Dance* (1968). In it Mitchell used *kalela*, "a popular 'tribal' dance on the Copperbelt of Northern Rhodesia . . . as a vehicle for a general enquiry into tribalism and some other features of social relationships among Africans in the towns" (1). All over the copper belt, teams of dancers performed every Sunday, drumming and singing before throngs of spectators. The team Mitchell observed in 1951 were all Bisa. The rank and file wore European clothing as their dance costumes (grey pants, singlets, and polished shoes). One dancer was dressed as a doctor, in a white tunic with red cross, and the one female dancer was dressed as a nurse. Their team "king" wore a dark suit, collar and tie, hat, and sunglasses. He officiated but did not dance. All the dancers were young manual workers who had come to the mines from two different Bisa chiefdoms. The team performed as if representing all Bisa against other tribes in the town in regular dance competitions. They sang in the lingua franca form of Bemba used in the towns of the copper belt. Many of the songs praised the Bisa and their land of origin. Others made fun of the other tribal groups in the area and commented satirically on the characteristics of tribal and urban life.

Mitchell set out to place this form of recreation in its social context. During this period the population living in any location was constantly changing, and much of Mitchell's analysis concerns the categories people used to identify and classify the strangers among whom they found themselves, with tribe of origin an important one. But in a survey of tribal classifications that investigated the respondents' views of the social distance of others, Mitchell found that fine categorical distinctions were made only with reference to tribes geographically close to the place of origin of the respondent. All others were lumped together in a simplified social/tribal "map" that reduced the many peoples in more distant areas into a few large politically dominant tribal categories. Thus, although Mitchell found that "ethnic distinctiveness" constituted the most significant category in day-to-day social interaction in the towns, he did not consider it the same phenomenon as tribal membership in the rural countryside. On the contrary, he argued that because so many different groups came in contact with each other, this "tribal" feature came to have an exaggerated importance in town that it lacked in rural areas where ethnic homogeneity, taken for granted, receded into the background.

Mitchell further developed the transformed meanings of town "tribalism" in a succinct historical sketch. He described the way the government and mining company administrations had at first set up a system of tribal representatives through whom they negotiated with the African workers. This framework soon proved inadequate in the mines. The structural opposition of interests between all Africans and their European managers was much more significant than any tribal differences among the Africans. Thus, the miners gave overwhelming support for the efforts of the African Mineworkers Union to get the tribal representative system abolished, an effort that eventually succeeded. Mitchell comments that "tribalism is still a significant category of social interaction within the field of African to African relationships . . . but it is not a relevant category in the field of Black-White relations" (1968, 34). But he is also clear that except for the dancing teams, tribalism in the copper belt did not form the basis for the organization of corporate groups (ibid., 42). It was simply a category of interaction in mediating social relationships "in what is predominantly a transient society" (ibid., 43). The industrial system, not the tribal system, represented the principal basis of existence in the copper belt (ibid., 44). "I contend," he wrote, "that the set of relationships among a group of tribesmen in their rural home is something very different from the set of relationships among the same group when they are transposed to an urban area" (Mitchell 1968, 44).

Mitchell saw clearly that the idea of "tribalism" was used to describe two very different phenomena, the nature of resident membership in a rural tribal community and a very important aspect— but by no means the only one— of an urban dweller's complex identity. In the copper belt towns, the place and culture of origin was highlighted by the presence of many others of different origins. But this ethnic mix existed in a social field in which a multiplicity of other characteristics also carried weight. The situation, the surround, and the setting redefined the meaning of the tribal. Unlike the Wilsons and the Mayers, Mitchell did not treat tribal connections and categories as a form of conservatism, a traditionalism in which fragments of the past were retained in a rapidly changing milieu. Mitchell saw that even the uses of what appeared to be tradition were new in the new industrial setting. The treatment of the tribal as a new form of ethnicity rather than as an old form of primitivity represented a significant advance.

Because the Mayers wrote at a later time and obviously had read much of the Rhodes-Livingstone group's work, one wonders why they did not avail themselves of Mitchell's sensible piece of sociologic. A partial reason, apart from theoretical differences, may be that the Mayers worked in an urban area where all of the Africans were Xhosa; consequently, they focused their attention on internal differences within one ethnic group. The Rhodes-Livingstone scholars conversely did their work in the copper belt mining towns, which were multiethnic from the start. In the copper belt, the anthropologists focused on the social and class consequences of the major division between African and European and the significant divisions between African and African. The anthropologists were more concerned with the bases of association and class than with the maintenance or fading of "tradition."

As Gluckman said in an oft-quoted passage, "An African townsman is a townsman, an African miner is a miner" (1961, 61; cited, for example, by Gutkind 1974, 31, and by Banton 1965, 134). (For a mild critique of the Gluckman formulation see Epstein 1967b.) The Rhodes-Livingstone group was acutely conscious of the dominant and privileged position of Europeans in relation to Africans and of the position of the town Africans as laborers. The ultimate control of urban organization did not rest in African hands; however, African reactions to government and mining-company policies certainly affected the way European structures developed and the way their policies were implemented.

Others besides the Rhodes-Livingstone group were engaged in this problematic. For those deeply occupied with contemporary social problems in Africa and the well-being of Africans, the pure, "barely touched by Europeans" African city was obviously not the general object of interest it had been for Miner. In 1956, Daryll Forde edited a collection of papers for UNESCO, *Social Implications of Urbanization and Industrialization in Africa*

South of the Sahara, in which the link with contemporary labor developments was pivotal. (For a recent overview of the history of *The African Worker* and a useful bibliography, see Freund 1988.) Urban anthropology was not being approached in only one mode.

Why Two Paradigms, "Tribe" and "Town"?

The centering of social anthropological theorizing on reconstructed "tribal" systems was eventually to pass. But for a time the structural-functional paradigm continued to be applied to rural peoples even as innovative, paradigm-shifting work was simultaneously going on in the towns. What the anthropologists did was to treat tribal typologies and urban realities as two entirely different domains of knowledge, more or less understood as analogous to two stages of social evolution and thus legitimately requiring different explanatory models.

This suggests some very interesting things about the history of social thought in anthropology. It shows that the most visible paradigms are not necessarily universally applied, even by their enthusiastic proponents. Quite separate and different streams of work often occur simultaneously, and these are deeply influenced by the history of various academic institutions, the history of a particular fieldwork region, and the history of the anthropological work done in that region (Fardon 1990). At mid-century it required only reclassification to accommodate quite inconsistent forms of academic knowledge without going to the mat in a fight about it. Given the connections between the dominance of structural-functional paradigms and the authoritative voices that spoke for them at Oxford and Cambridge, it is no wonder that there was no confrontational struggle— indeed, the inconsistencies were invisible to many of the scholars.

But it also shows that in less prestigious centers, the research institutes in Africa, for example, innovative ideas could be cultivated. Part of the excitement was surely the breaking of new theoretical ground with a team of colleagues engaged in parallel endeavors. In this regard, the distance from the metropole was no doubt liberating in two ways: (1) the centers of orthodoxy were not close by and contact with them was discontinuous, and (2) the research institutes were very close to the sites of fieldwork. The institutes were in Africa, whose own changing history was the catalyst for these new approaches. Recent critics, in their zeal to demonstrate the shortcomings of structural functionalism, have often forgotten that the comparative study of reconstructed "tribal" types was by no means the only subject of interest in anthropological work in Africa even in the late 1930s, 1940s, and 1950s, let alone thereafter. Latent in the very idea of the precolonial "tribal society" was its contrast with another kind of social world that had invaded it: a large-scale, technically advanced, complex, heterogeneous one in which the active presence of colonial administrators, settler commercial enterprises, missionaries, and local labor recruitment had to be taken into account.

Obviously, the anthropologists concerned with the colonial presence and the changes it brought knew very well that African transformations did not begin with the colonial period. Archeological and historical evidence made it plain that change had been continuous. Long before and well after the centuries of the slave trade, powerful African kingdoms sought to expand their influence. Long-distance trade routes were extended and fought over. Substantial population movements altered the social landscape, and vast economic and cultural changes took place. The detailed record of that history and that of the colonial period has been filled out in many recent works. These studies often draw on anthropological understandings of recent African communities to amplify the reconstruction of the past (see, for example, Chanock 1985; Cohen 1972, 1977, 1989, 1992; Comaroff 1985; Comaroff and Comaroff 1991; Feierman 1974, 1990; Goody 1971; Harms 1981, 1987; Hopkins 1973; Iliffe 1969, 1979, 1987; Kopytoff 1987; Miers and Kopytoff 1977; Richards 1985). But well before the post mid-century spate of rich historical work, there was a general awareness in anthropology of Africa's past. Even in the highest period of structural-functional theorizing, many an ethnography started with a sketch of what was known of local precolonial history. But writing such historical introductions was considered an activity quite distinct from the witnessing of change through ethnographic observation. History and anthropology were treated by many as two entirely different kinds of academic enterprise with different objectives and different techniques. Some, such as Claude Lévi-Strauss, still hold this view. It is in the light of that premise that the efforts of a substantial segment of the profession to address the rural-urban link, to look straight at the new Africa, constituted an important step forward. It was an opening up of ethnography to the contemporary and the nontraditional as focal topics. For that group of anthropologists, the liveliness of the contemporary scene in the very midst of transformation was patently a legitimate object for anthropological inspection.

As we have seen, the model of the rural-urban "continuum" often had imbedded within it the concept that rural-urban comparisons were a concrete embodiment of the process of change, that large parts of the past were preserved in the rural, folk life, that urbanism was characterized by the replacement of those characteristics. The use of the term *conservative* to characterize the "tribal" African was one manifestation of that idea (see, for example, Gulliver's use of the term, 1969).

Thus, the conception of the colonial city as a center and source of modernity influenced the contrastive way the "tribal" or rural itself was constructed. The fact is, of course, that conditions in the countryside changed at the same time that cities grew, often in related ways. But the "tribal" *model* was not changing, since its goal was a reconstruction of a precolonial African "type," not the recording of a full, unexpurgated account of changing events and practices in the countryside at the time of fieldwork. To be sure, collective cultural differences were important then, and they have continued significance in Africa to this day. In many parts of the continent, tribal or ethnic identities have ongoing social and political salience. But this should not be mistaken for an unchanging traditionalism.

Historical processes of transformation have involved all of Africa. The question of whether these changes have been apparent and noted has always depended on the knowledge, attitudes, and objectives of the beholders.

It is significant that the very same anthropologists from the Rhodes-Livingstone Institute who began working in towns produced two kinds of "tribal" ethnographies. They wrote reconstructions in the classical manner (see, for example, Colson and Gluckman 1951), and they also wrote, in an entirely different mode, contemporary descriptions of the changes they actually saw in the field (see Gluckman 1941; Colson 1960a, 1971; and Colson and Scudder 1975). The balance had shifted between attention to the customary and attention to what was changing.

Networks, Associations, and Classes

For those working in the towns, the intense preoccupation of "tribal" anthropology with kinship as the fundamental key both to individual status and to group formation was necessarily replaced by a much more open approach. By no means did all migrants have families with them. Some had relatives in town, but many did not. Kinship was not a sufficient medium of analysis. Other categories of relationship were critically important. The question became one of investigating those ties.

New approaches were initiated from two contrasting points of departure. One approach stressed organized collectivities. Anthropologists studied voluntary associations and class categories to find out how they were formed and how they operated (Little 1965; Lloyd 1966; Meillassoux 1968). The other approach proceeded from individuals and followed them into their various life settings (Mitchell 1969). This produced a very rich and innovative set of analyses of networks, situations, and transactions, objects of knowledge very different from the "whole cultures" described in the "tribal" mode. A new conception emerged of the relationship between a person and a sociocultural milieu.

The "tribal" model had concentrated on the social norms that were thought to govern the social behavior of individuals and to dominate their lives. Instead, the analysis of urban networks used an individual-centered approach. The chains of relationships that radiated out from a particular person, the people he/she knew and had dealings with, and the friends of those friends and so on, constituted a personal network. What quickly came to be of interest was not just the existence of links in the chain but the nature of the contacts between the persons in the network, the content of their transactions. As soon as these began to be studied, the fact that choices existed among norms and that people sometimes conformed and sometimes did not— in short, that they were given to manipulating the normative system in their own interest— could hardly be excluded from consideration. That led to a new orientation toward fieldwork, centered on agency, on individuals as active constructors of aspects of their own lives. The "cultural and social system" orientation was not discarded, but "the system," such as it was, came to be seen as a much more complex product of events of interaction. The culture and the social system of urban Africa looked as if it were continuously negotiated, made and remade, sometimes reiterated, sometimes modified or replaced. Time entered the picture. Networks were built and used, and a sequence of transactions took place over time. There was no going back to a conception of a purely repetitive, endlessly reproduced, fixed cultural system in the presence of such ethnographic preoccupations. The techniques of network study generated in urban Africa by Mitchell (1969) and on transactions by Kapferer (1972, 1976) and also applied to a different milieu by Gulliver (1971) were an important force in the reorientation of social anthropology away from the structural-functional model.

Even by 1960, it was evident that social anthropology was moving along new paths. What had rung the death knell of the structural-functional paradigm? A number of factors coincided. One was the post–World War II momentum toward the decolonization of Africa, with all of its nontribal, nontraditional implications. A second circumstance was that with the passage of time it had become more and more apparent that Radcliffe-Brown's "scientific" goal of discovering social laws through ethnographic comparisons was a promise that would never be realized. When, in 1946, Evans-Pritchard succeeded Radcliffe-Brown as professor at Oxford, a new generation had come to control the British university scene. The earlier era gradually came to a close. (Similar changes of direction were experienced in postwar sociology, with concomitant bursts of innovative study.) The third element was surely the expanding influence of the kind of present-oriented, actor-focused, ethnographic work of which the studies produced at the Rhodes-Livingstone Institute were probably the most important initiating experimental example.

In Sanjek's review of the state of urban anthropology in the 1980s, he referred back to these "landmark studies in the urban anthropology of the 1950s to 1970s period" with considerable respect (1990b, 165; see also Hannerz 1980; and Coquery-Vidrovitch 1991, which cited not just anthropological works but sociological, historical, and geographical writings in a broad overview of the process of urbanization in Africa). Sanjek noted the recurrence of some of the original themes in the 1980s, such as labor migration and ethnicity (Eades 1987; Mitchell 1987; Nolan 1986; Obbo 1980; Oppong 1983). But they are treated in a different way. A substantial differentiation of topics is also evident. Urban settings have become the locus for the same broad variety of specialized studies that characterize present-day anthropology in general. Sanjek (1990b) notes, for example, healing practices (Wyllie 1980; Mullings 1984); the production and marketing of cloth (Goody 1982a; Launay 1982; Wagner 1982); apprenticeship, child labor, and child fostering (Goody 1982b; Schildkrout 1981, 1986a); household workers (Cock 1980; Hansen 1989; Sanjek 1990a); class formation (Lubeck 1986; MacGaffey 1987); politics, elite culture, and popular culture (Barnes 1986; Cohen 1981; Hannerz 1987); and religious sects and practices (Besmer 1983; MacGaffey 1983). The theme of socially constructed gender differences generally permeates much of this recent work but is the special focus of some studies (Sanjek 1983; Schildkrout 1983, 1986b).

Two major changes in anthropology are reflected in the urban work in Africa reviewed both by Sanjek 1990b and by Coquery-Vidrovitch 1988, 1991. One change is that ethnographic research in cities today is not overly concerned with the countryside/town divide as the epitomy of two types of social system. For the writers of the earlier period, 1950s to 1970s, the difference tribal/urban was a theoretical and methodological preoccupation. It is no longer. A model confined to two crude types is overly simple and too ahistorical to be of much use. Some of this rethinking is attributable to changes in the countryside itself, some of it to a quite different, much more nuanced conception of the great variety of present-day sociocultural forms in Africa and the history that produced them. The other clear change is that social anthropology has developed into a field of many distinct topical subspecializations. Recent ethnographic monographs, whether urban or rural, have consequently tended to define the boundaries of the research problems they address in terms of thematic issues, rather than trying to depict the "whole way of life" of any group of people. This shift of focus marks a general change in anthropology as a discipline, a change that is now highly visible in the work in Africa.

African Independence and Anthropological Specialization, 1960–90

Introduction: Academia Questions Itself, or, the Snake Bites Its Own Tail

CONFIDENCE in the value of the anthropological project was surely the typical mood of the anthropologists who studied Africa in the 1930–60 period. They had no skepticism about the utility of their work. They had no doubt that fieldwork produced better answers and a better understanding of African life, thought, and issues than was available to missionaries, administrators, and settlers. The anthropologists also believed that the expansion of knowledge was itself an unmitigated good, whether or not it had any obvious practical application. Each decade produced new insights and revisions of the theses of earlier works. Disagreements certainly existed, but rather than reject all previous contributions out of hand because they did not include the latest perspective, there was a strong sense that the discipline was cumulative, learning, moving forward. Some of the anthropologists in the Durkheimian tradition struggled to make the field more of a science, to instill a discipline of comparisons that could produce sociological generalizations. Others, in the Evans-Pritchard tradition, were more inclined toward humanistic understandings. Still others wanted to develop modes of analysis suitable for the Africa of towns and migrant labor. But these and other differences apart, the anthropologists of this period thought of themselves as empathic friends of Africans and accurate observers of the situation. Moreover, many anthropologists saw themselves as unequivocally on the African side of the controversial issues of the colonial period. They considered themselves knowledgeable go-betweens, occasional intervenors on behalf of Africans in their dealings with the administration.

Thirty-some years after independence, an entirely different mood has overtaken the academic enterprise. It has experienced a number of attacks, internal and external, that have not merely been revisionist but have shaken the foundations. Today, Africanist anthropologists can seldom conceive of themselves as needed spokespersons for Africans. For one thing, Africans speak for themselves in many arenas. For another, African affairs have now attracted the interest of a multiplicity of disciplines. A diverse collection of interpreters and interpretations are at the ready. Anthropology today finds itself just one of many interested parties.

African intellectuals (both expatriates and those who continue to live in Africa) want to control more of the action. And in the Euro-American scene, the interested parties, academics and others (governments, the World Bank, nongovernmental organizations, and churches) have often disagreed and vied among themselves for control of the field of discourse about Africa. After two decades of political infighting, an Africanist trying to see the agenda for the future in an optimistic light asked and tried to answer a gloomy question, "Who Needs African Studies?" (Staniland 1983).

There have always been some who tried to make common cause, who tried to locate a list of objectives common to all those involved in African studies, to find the common ground. But what appears nominally to be the same strategy can be used for very different and divisive purposes. In his 1983 article, Staniland began by describing the then ongoing state of turbulence in African studies in the United States. "The crisis has been protracted and conflict at times has been intense (notably the African Studies Association's 1969 conference in Montreal when the proceedings were interrupted by black radicals and the entire meeting was given over to argument regarding the loyalties and priorities that Africanist scholars should adopt). . . . Africanists as a group have not shown much interest in the structure of the debate itself (as distinct from the righteousness of their individual positions)" (77).

On the question of who has legitimate claims on the project of understanding African concerns and situations, M. G. Smith offers insight. A Jamaican anthropologist trained in Britain, he worked both in northern Nigeria and in the Caribbean, and he served as professor of anthropology at UCLA, at University College, London, and at Yale. In the midst of the turmoil of the sixties and seventies, when there were occasional, but vituperative, objections to whites teaching African topics, he used to say quite simply, "One does not have to be a triangle to understand geometry" (personal communication). Edward Said, who in the late 1970s made one of the strongest academic attacks on Western cultural biases in the recent literature, also said categorically, "I certainly do not believe the limited proposition that only a black can write about blacks, a Muslim about Muslims, and so forth" (1979, 322). The orientalist critique is one thing, racialism another thing entirely.

But it is evident that since the 1960s anthropologists from the advanced industrial countries have found themselves in an uncomfortable state of political self-consciousness. Anthropology has come to understand itself as a maverick branch of the intellectual life of the richest and most powerful half of the world. Anyone from the industrial "North" working in Africa today never forgets for a moment (nor do Africans let them forget) that they have come to visit and study the affairs of people in less powerful, less economically privileged countries. A dramatic wave of reflection on this political and economic asymmetry, how it has come about, what it means now, its present inescapability for Africans and outsiders alike, and the way it invades interaction is the frame within which the anthropology of today and of the past thirty years is best understood.

In the first period of celebration after independence, a certain optimism existed in many quarters about the possibility of accelerating economic development in Africa, the possibility of gradually redressing the North-South asymmetry, and there were classical economic theories about how that "development" could be brought about. Those hopes were eroded in the years that followed. The failures gave world-systems theory and dependency theory a wide academic audience. These had a number of proponents and forms, but the notion basically was that the underdevelopment of "peripheral" parts of the world and the advanced development of the "center" were not disconnected and independent historical accidents. The thesis was that they must be seen as linked parts of a single system: the world capitalist system. In this interpretation, the maintenance of the asymmetry between the center and the periphery were seen to be in the interest of the center. Marxist interpretations of the African situation represented a variant of this theme that puts its emphasis on African systems of production and reproduction. The Marxists had to overcome the legacy of evolutionary models, the notion that capitalist production and traditional subsistence production were two entirely separate and different types. The model developed to link the two addressed the articulation of these two modes of production. It argued that capitalist production preserved "traditional" African rural systems for good economic reasons. In rural villages, the preservation of "tradition" and the maintenance of a subsistence economy helped to meet the costs of reproducing the labor force. As a consequence, those costs did not require higher wages for the laborers. (For a very clear discussion of these economic models and an enumeration of their shortcomings as well as a useful bibliographical review, see Cooper 1981.) The debates over development, dependency, and modes of production necessarily jarred and disturbed the interpretations of many anthropologists, whether or not they accepted the full implications of the models.

Thus, it is plain that the asymmetry between "developed" and "underdeveloped" worlds was the most pervasive theme that permeated African studies after 1960. Other forms of self-examination and self-criticism branched out from this foundational one, and some that originally had other sources soon attached themselves to the asymmetrical base as to a magnet. These additional critiques are many and various, a substantial number generated in academic fields other than anthropology, many mixing careful logic with wild polemic in equal quantities (indigestible mixture). The sorting-out of these diverse criticisms requires a calm temperament and a lot of time.

Right or wrong, distorting or incisive, the attacks and uncertainties are part of the present African studies scene in academe, which is a highly politicized one. Consequently, the competition about who is to define the "real" situation in Africa often takes a very bitter turn. One can find crude accusations that anthropology itself has been complicit in creating the present political-economic asymmetry; hence, all anthropology is morally tainted. Equally often, one can find the allegation that anthropology has, for its own theoretical purposes (and in the service of the exploitative purposes of others), invented an Africa that does not exist, constituting another form of immorality, the distortion of truth. Both are gross, overdramatized, formulaic exaggerations.

But the conundrums to which such statements purport to be answers are anything but silly. The question how to understand cumulative historical causality has long been the focus of intellectual debate, from Marx to Weber to Braudel and beyond. And the issue is plainly anything but closed. The other question, equally complex and unresolved, is how to understand the creation of collective ideologies and to assess intellectual responsibility for them, how to reconceive the problems of culture and agency, ideology and practice, and how to integrate these with the study of history.

If ethnographers necessarily interpret what they witness, and they do (and must), does that mean that the communicated result is always in some degree a reconstructed, reshaped representation, altered by the culture and temperament of anthropologists and affected by the historical moment in which they are writing? How much reality exists that independent observers of different cultural origins might notice in the same way? Has the tumultuous political context of the postcolonial world affected not only the locales of ethnographic observation and the choice of subject matter but also determined the idioms of controversy?

The "colonial mentality" argument was one of the earliest themes in a series of major post–1960s attacks on anthropology from within. These attacks found much the same audience as did the contention that independence had not delivered what it had seemed to promise, that postcolonial African economies were neocolonial, i.e., instances of continued economic domination without formal administrative control. Thus, as one looks at subsequent critiques it becomes clear that the colonial mentality attack had implications that went far beyond its initial focus. It gave relative weight to the power of frameworks of thought over the appearance of facts. It was a statement about the nonautonomy of intellection. Some of the elaborations of Antonio Gramsci's ideas about hegemony and about domination through cultural supremacy also percolated into anthropology. The unwilling and unwitting captivity of consciousness has also recently engaged Africanists interested in the historical products of the European-African "dialogue," for example, John and Jean Comaroff (1991).

Feminists raised even more persuasive objections about systematic absences and omissions in the anthropological record. Where were the women in the standard ethnographies? For years, women's lives, women's activities— their words and thoughts— hardly figured in ethnographic work. With a few notable exceptions, fieldwork was about men, and the male perspective governed. But it was not seen as a male perspective. It was seen as "the society," and it seemed "natural" that men ran it.

Some of this bias was no doubt for lack of access. In many social settings it was difficult, if not impossible, for male anthropologists to approach women, let alone come to know them well, and most anthropologists were male. But the fact that they could not easily talk to the women at their field sites was surely not the only reason they did not consider local attitudes toward gender politically significant. In the classical period, most (but not all) of the women anthropologists in the African field (and as we have seen, there were a number of them) were as much focused on the male perspective as were their male colleagues and mentors. Women's lives were seen as determined by their roles as daughters, wives, and mothers of men. Women were adjuncts to the men. Over the years, the dilemmas of understanding raised by the gender issue have become more varied and more numerous and more intense.

Some allege that "feminist ethnography has focused either on setting the record straight about women or on revising anthropological categories (for example, the nature/culture opposition). It has not produced either unconventional forms of writing or a developed reflection on ethnographic textuality as such" (Clifford and Marcus 1986, 20–21). But surely whether focused on textuality or not, the implications of gender-conscious ethnography have been quite radical and far-reaching. That story is not yet finished. Perhaps the most dismaying aspect of it has been the irrefutable evidence that there was a general blind spot, which raises the question of how many more such blind spots there might be and gives encouragement to those who would cast every possible doubt on the objectivity of any anthropological observation. But there is a huge polemic leap from recognizing the existence of an important blind spot to arguing that there is a total incapacity to see. The jump seems unjustified and needlessly destructive.

Ethnographic work is an inevitably flawed attempt to learn. It uses a human being as its instrument of discovery and subsequent communication. All the shortcomings that attend the two steps of this method must be acknowledged. But there are many close-quarter inquiries that cannot be conducted in any other way. There is much reason to be conscious of the limits of awareness and presentation that this double technique entails, but there is no reason to forgo the method. There are no substitutes for this form of access to otherwise unknowable material.

Self-consciousness about such methodological matters has now produced two major modalities in anthropological discourse, one that speaks largely through the production of ethnographic writings and the other a kind of critical meta-anthropology that speaks through its commentary on the ethnographic writings of others. That meta-anthropology treats ethnographies as texts to be deconstructed and reinterpreted. Parts of the literary deconstructionist strategy of Jacques Derrida has made its way into the analysis of ethnography. Thus, not only are writers of ethnography today exhorted to worry about their unconscious biases and to take every measure possible to uncover them, but they are also put on notice that they are not in full control of the meaning of the texts they produce. Their readers will not be passive recipients of so-called facts but rather will read their own understandings into the text. It is generally recognized that like other literature, "ethnographies are susceptible to multiple interpretations" (Clifford and Marcus 1986, 120). James Clifford comments that "Much of our knowledge about other cultures must now be seen as contingent, the problematic outcome of intersubjective dialogue, translation, and projection. . . . Once the ethnographic process is accorded its full complexity . . . what formerly seemed to be empirical/interpretive accounts of generalized cultural facts . . . now appear as just one level of allegory" (ibid., 109). He acknowledges that such accounts may be complex and truthful and that they may be susceptible to refutation, but he argues that there is no way "to separate the factual from the allegorical in cultural accounts" (ibid., 119). Yet he also says in a moralizing vein, "We struggle to confront and take responsibility for our systematic construction of others and of ourselves through others. . . . If we are condemned to tell stories we cannot control, may we not, at least, tell stories we believe to be true" (ibid., 121).

Needless to say, this style of commentary has by now profoundly affected ethnographic reading and may soon be seen to have permeated the process of writing. A positive result would be to induce more candor, a certain humility, a little more inhibition of the ethnographer's will to generalize from limited information. One hopes, though, that this will not inhibit the continued production of colorful instances of speculative interpretation provided they are acknowledged to be such. The bad news is that such a stance may encourage excesses of improvisation, justify free-form fictionalization masquerading as fact, and, worse, discourage verifying inquiries that could confirm or refute what appears to be the case. The question of verifiability and falsifiability surely should never be far from the surface in the ethnographic quest. There are more and less responsible interpretations. Careful work is careful work. It takes a long time, it does not always read as well as mythologizing, but it is worth doing. There is a difference between a work of fiction and an ethnography, a difference in purpose and a difference in mode of construction. Those differences should not be lost, even now that we know that when treated as literary texts the two have more in common than might once have been supposed.

Not surprisingly, meta-anthropological commentary has become a common topic of theoretical debate in social anthropology as a whole. It is a game at which any number can play, whatever the geographical area in which they work. By contrast to this wide interest in the textual-theoretical critique, there is a much more circumscribed interest in regionally based ethnographic material. That domain remains much more the territory of the thematic or area specialist (Fardon 1990). Each approach involves a different take on the selective production of knowledge and the vagaries of that process.

The secondary critical commentary is no small sideline. It is a substantial growth industry. Much easier to do than fieldwork, it can be produced by sojourns in the library. It does not involve taking malaria pills, walking many dusty miles, and being directly confronted with the dilemmas and envy of living Africans. In its most literary forms, the critique is barely concerned with the accuracy of the ethnographer's description or with its significance as a record of current history. Instead, the preoccupation is with the thought, the mind-set, the approach, of the ethnographer as manifested in the ethnographer's textual representation of the Other. In some hands, the ethnographer's thought is then used as evidence of the general cultural biases of the West. The logic leaps from one to all.

When the rhetoric so intertwines a moral/political reproach in its textual analysis, it becomes plain that a political statement was the underlying purpose of the literary exercise. This reproach of the West for having achieved a privileged state has conventional— one might even say generic— forms, easily and often imitated. For example, it is now commonplace to borrow from Michel Foucault the technique of characterizing particular ways of writing as part of a contemporary "discourse" of power, as if the discourse were the cause and the power the effect. In the specific historical instances Foucault describes with some relish, the particular uses of "power" on which he dwells tend to strike current readers as repugnant and shocking, whether he is talking about the treatment of criminals or the practical application of ideas of insanity. But "discourse," even in the broad ambiguous sense in which Foucault used it (linking concepts, statements, and practices) is not an altogether satisfactory causal explanation. It describes a temporally unitary nexus, not a sequential dynamic.

When Africanist anthropologists are accused of contributing to the "discourse" of power through the very practice of their profession, they react with deep personal and intellectual discomfort. Of course, they find themselves inextricably linked to the prosperous side of the world. They are stuck with their identities through birth, culture, training, and citizenship and through the otherwise welcome financing of their research projects. They are uncomfortable with the idea that they are, by sheer accident of identity, associated with the policies and practices, real and imagined, past and present, that are alleged by political critics to emanate from their side of the world. Anthropologists often try to disconnect by expending a remarkable amount of print subtly— or crudely— dissociating themselves from well-known manifestations of Euro-American global power. These efforts attempt in part to please what is conceived to be the African audience, in part the polemically inclined domestic one, which is quite noisy in parts of academe.

When it comes to the identity issue, African intellectuals appear at first glance to have a certain advantage. On the face of it, they should not have to work as hard to distance themselves from a first-world identity, because that is not the part of the world they come from. But in fact, to the extent that they are members of an elite, trained by their education to work in the milieu of Anglo-European languages and practices, some feel all the more obliged to distance themselves from a tradition to which they are closely tied but about which they feel politically ambivalent. At the same time that they want intellectual recognition from the Western intellectual academy, they want to enjoy their freedom to attack it. The conflict embedded in this multiple identity is palpable in novels (see Miller 1990 on West African literature in French). In disciplines other than comparative literature, African intellectuals are well situated to rail against what they see as the misreadings of outsiders and to propose their own counterversions of the "real" Africa and its "real" history. Indeed, Miller, speaking of the complaints of the philosopher Paulin Hountondji, says, "Hountondji shows how the division of labor has been unequal, with the highly valued role of theorizer belonging almost exclusively to Westerners, while Africans are confined to the gathering of raw information. Africa provides materials (like palm oil or literary texts), which European institutes process into finished commodities (like Palmolive soap or works of criticism of African literature)" (1990, 2). An intellectual recolonization argument is not hard to find in this polemic that wants to reclaim the last word on Africa as the exclusive property of Africans.

To get the flavor of some of these debates, one might read the complex, indigestible, and highly opinionated review of many African issues written by a Zairean who lives in the United States, V. Y. Mudimbe's *The Invention of Africa* (1988). He is not an anthropologist, and he has his own ideas of what anthropology is about. Because he comments repeatedly on anthropological works, has a certain Foucaultian slant, and is strongly focused on philosophical and theological questions about reality, his work touches a number of themes that impinge on Africanist anthropology today. (See also Van der Geest and Kirby 1992).

As Mudimbe's title suggests, his book is about the importance for Africa of the motivated and constructed nature of knowledge. He is concerned with something he calls "Africanity." There is a real question about whether a continentwide essence of Africanness exists, given the great variety of languages, cultures, occupations, and classes on that huge continent. Mudimbe is very much aware of this diversity as an analytic problem but treats in special detail those theorizings that have proposed universal interpretations of human thought (for example, Lévi-Strauss 1966), unitary ideas of Africa (Tempels 1959), or ideas about negritude and Pan-Africanism. Mudimbe sets up African concepts of a unitary essence of Africanity in a kind of symmetrical opposition against a supposedly generalized Western idea of African primitivity. Needless to say, he is less than charitable about what he calls a "primitivist anthropology" (1988, 193). He does think that a reconstituted anthropology could be a good thing, however: "The question I am dealing with is one which would account for the possibility of anthropological knowledge, and its meaning for the foundation of both Africanist discourses and African gnosis. I am proposing to formulate it through a critical synthesis of Foucault's thesis on the last archaeological rupture in Western epistemology, a brief interpretation of Lévi-Strauss's notion of *savage mind,* and finally a plea for the importance of the subject in social sciences; a subject that structuralism too easily pretends to have killed" (ibid., 23).

In the course of his exposition, Mudimbe covers an enormous and varied bibliography, heavily but not exclusively francophone. Although he returns again and again to anthropology, it is by no means his only focus. He is almost equally occupied with Christianity, with the missionary project, with African religions, with philosophy, with history, with Marxism, and with African nationalism, and he argues with everyone he quotes. Ideas about Africanity constitute his main subject matter; he does not address the concrete social and economic situation of Africa and Africans. This leads him to concentrate on the kind of anthropology that focuses on "modes of thought," and he hardly addresses the large anthropological literature that raises very different issues. Mudimbe basically seeks to show that some models portray African "modes of thought" as inherently inferior to others and to assert that such contentions are entirely wrong, a thesis with which no reputable Africanist would quarrel. Mudimbe ends with a plea for listening to African versions of self and history, including attending to the ideological strategies of proponents of negritude, black personality, and Pan-Africanist movements, paying attention to ethnophilosophy in examining African and Christian theology, and to the project of rewriting history, of "reinventing the African past" (ibid., 194). The result is far from an easy read. Even when one disagrees with some of the theses put forward, however, one cannot but be impressed by the audacity involved in attempting to encompass such a vast panorama of perspectives all at once.

Mudimbe draws on and argues with the writings of many others, African and non-African, but the reading and synthesis are very much Mudimbe's own. It would be a mistake to suppose that all African intellectuals focus on the same set of issues or that they all share his opinions. The Mudimbe book is interesting for present purposes because its collage of opinions contains bits and pieces from most of the major waves of critical theorizing of the past thirty-some years, and these are interposed with Mudimbe's philosophical and theological preoccupations.

Five waves of critical theorizing have been noted here. None of these has originated in anthropology, but they have all strongly affected the discipline, as they have African studies in general. The first critique is the attack on colonialism, no longer, of course, in its old political form because that is in fact long since over, but in the form of "neocolonial" relationships and ideas or metaphoric frameworks of "recolonization." The second is the global economy critique, which has many different versions and subversions, including classical economic, dependency oriented, Marxist, world systems, and others. The third is the gender critique, which prescribes a reunderstanding of the literature, a recasting of ethnographic observation, and a redesign of the ethnographic imagination to repair the distortions of the past and prevent their repetition. The fourth argues that all reading and discussion should be rethought in light of the Foucaultian discourse of power. The fifth is the postmodern, literary-critical understanding of the problematic of meaning, which for the anthropologist is associated with all the many dilemmas of dialogue, translation, representation, and textual reading that have always existed but have now become especially visible. Given the endless repetitions by anthropologists of what have become conventional criticisms of anthropology, one cannot help but notice that this is a time in academic life when the lines between high seriousness, self-satire, and political self-interest can sometimes be difficult to draw.

Meanwhile, despite the spate of critiques, the serious ethnographic work continues. The rest of this book will briefly summarize the myriad forms that practical ethnographic work in Africa has taken from 1960 to the 1990s and note the links with earlier studies. Thus, there will be a certain amount of tacking back and forth from earlier to later monographs, because anthropologists who wrote before 1960 continued to work after Africa's political independence and work done in the colonial period continued to influence subsequent scholarship. The academic context in which this ethnographic work has been carried on since 1960 has been less than peaceful, but it is surprising how little the debates seem to have limited recent productivity in Africanist anthropology. In fact, the passionate arguments in the background may well have stimulated the eventual exploration of new topics and inspired experiments with presentation. One sees ample signs of both today.

Dated Compendia and Subsequent Waves of Innovation

Four grand themes have animated social anthropology from the beginning: explorations of modes of thought, modes of production, modes of organization, and modes of transformation. These four have been approached quite differently at different periods. An accelerating process of redefinition has been especially marked since the 1950s. The fourth theme, which used to be a pale shadow, now dominates much of the field and pervades the first three. The question which of these themes should be given primacy in ethnographic description and which should be treated as secondary has depended partly on the kind of material being analyzed but even more on who happens to be the author of the analysis. For example, for Mary Douglas (1963, 1966, 1970, 1973) the categories of thought and their logic are what matter. For Claude Meillassoux (1964a, 1981) everything else hinges on the relations of production. For Meyer Fortes (1945, 1949b, 1970), much else followed from lineage organization. And when M. G. Smith (1960, 1974, 1978) wrote about the history of African kingdoms and the politics of African pluralism, the nature of their corporate organization was the key to the system. And for those who use a historically informed paradigm, such as John and Jean Comaroff (1985, 1991), Ivan Karp (1978), and I (1986, 1987), process and transformation (or active reiteration) inform.

Causal primacy or, at the very least, superior analytic utility, is often imputed to one or another element in these thematic domains. But there are, of course, many other productive ways to mix, match, and reclassify the data. The four grand categories are not mutually exclusive and are far from the only way to divide up the problems of analysis. The diverse possibilities have become increasingly evident in the ethnographic work of recent decades. Earlier conventions of ethnographic presentation (which were not very rigid to begin with) have been progressively opened up to more and more variation and experimentation.

In the same period, changes in the organization of academe itself have had a direct impact on African studies. Today, not only are there far more social anthropologists than before, but this enlarged profession has divided itself into many topical subspecialties. The general monograph that aims to describe the total way of life of a particular group of people is no longer the favorite product of academic industry. Ethnographic description is much more likely to focus on a particular issue and to candidly examine some small subgroup of persons, not a whole ethnic group. To give a few recent examples, monographs have appeared on family and household in a particular community, on a religious cult and its followers in a particular region, on particular art traders in certain West African urban markets, and the like. It is evident that the boundaries of tribe no longer constitute the paramount definers of subject matter. Ethnographers today are more candid about the limits of what they have actually seen or been told and are more cautious about generalizing from limited data than they used to be, when it was assumed that if you knew one community of a tribal or ethnic group, you knew them all.

Cross-cutting the present multiplicity of specialized local studies are a variety of theoretical subthemes, models, and critiques that appear and reappear in many topical settings. Thus, for example, a preoccupation with the situation of women may surface in very diverse ethnographic frames from marketing to widowhood, or an interest in the symbolism of the body may present itself in ethnomedicine or in a discussion of political imagery. Many such radical severings, innovations and recombinations have revised the categories of study and opened new topics.

The most pervasive reshaping of Africanist anthropology has emerged directly from the African scene itself. Obvious changes in the situation of Africans have forced more and more anthropologists to treat African transformations as a prime object of analysis. Whatever their particular field of specialization, anthropologists find that they must consider history past and history now in the making as part of their domain of inquiry.

The inescapable awareness that the Africa being observed is not standing still, not simply repeating its past, has deeply affected the definition of the ethnographic project. Questions are being raised about the state of knowledge of the people being studied, about the intentions and the choices of individuals, about their consciousness and sense of identity, about the effects of the decisions of the powerful and of the apparently powerless, and about the consequences of distant events. Traditional patterns of cultural and social constraint are by no means the only topic of interest.

As one might expect, a place in which some of these multiple changes in the discipline and in its analytic object are evident is in state-of-the-art writing. Until the period of independence, in addition to the ever-accumulating number of monographs, anthropologists repeatedly attempted to sum up the total anthropological knowledge of indigenous Africa. Enthusiasm for this kind of reference work inevitably waned as the theoretical interest in tribal system comparisons itself faded. Some early works that are no longer particularly useful include Herskovits's pioneering "culture area" papers (1930) and Seligman's *Races of Africa* (1957). In his state-of-the-art summary, Gulliver cites critically a German version of the culture-area approach that was published by Bauman et al. in 1943 (Gulliver 1965, 79). Another rejected early synthesis was the *Kulturkreis* approach, which is now generally discredited, although an interest in diffusion as historical fact continues (Ankermann 1905). By far the most respected assemblage of such information was the multivolume *Ethnographic Survey of Africa* started in 1950 under the aegis of Daryll Forde and the International African Institute. It remains a useful resource but a very dated one. (For the now conventional critique of its "tribal" approach, see Tonkin 1990.)

A later, overambitious attempt to compress everything into one reference book was Murdock's *Africa: Its Peoples and Their Culture History* (1959). Both the classifications and the interpretations found in Murdock's volume must be approached with caution, because they are by no means uniformly reliable.

African Independence

Murdock's work on Africa was an offshoot of the Human Relations Area Files, an enormous compendium of world cultural information that aspired to put in one huge accessible file with a common index all that existed in hundreds of ethnographic works. Murdock was no Africanist but rather an industrious compiler and classifier with a high faith in statistical measures. His was something of a "social genome" project. He wanted to identify all the critical elements that constituted social systems and then wanted to demonstrate the frequency of their occurrence in patterns. He had hoped to substantiate statistically the existence of cultural regularities through cross-cultural comparison, to replace speculations about integrated systems, however brilliant, with more "scientifically" substantiated generalizations about recurring associations.

The fact that this project fell far short of its ambitions demonstrated once again the remarkable complexity and subtlety of the data. The combinations and permutations of cultural characteristics, the conceptions of kinship, the symbolic structures, the ritual cycles, and the mythic explanations were immense in number and did not neatly match variations in the modes of production, the frameworks of exchange, or the constructions of political organization. Although some regularities surely existed, the neat typologies that had been expected did not emerge. The types were tribes, supposedly separate and distinct peoples and cultures. The typologizing did not and could not cope with the many known centuries of upheaval in African history; the very considerable contact among African peoples (let alone their contacts with outsiders); the migrations, large and small, that repeatedly characterized life on that continent; and the capacity of ideas, techniques, and objects to travel from hand to hand and from mind to mind and, indeed, to be reinvented. The task of making sense of whatever regularities exist in the complex amalgams that constitute the cultures of African peoples still tantalizes anthropologists, but from the 1960s on these were increasingly addressed in terms of specialized themes— religion, economy, law, kinship, gender, "modes of thought," and the like.

All of the earlier compendial works sought to identify and compare what were treated as the distinct "ethnic" or "tribal" groups of Africa conceived in terms of a pre-colonial way of life. (See, for example, Gulliver 1965, in which he says, "The 'natural' unit of study for the anthropologist in Africa has been the tribe"— not the "tribe" under colonial rule but the "tribe" *tout simple* [65].) But in fact, by 1960, the meaning of the "tribal" in Africa had come to be seen as a complex political fact. Detribalization was part of the nationalist discourse of many African leaders. For anthropologists, the existence and form of the precolonial "tribe" and its colonial reconstruction had come to be seen as subject matter for historical research and questioning, not as an unchanged and taken-for-granted institution amenable to ethnographic observation. Moreover, even during the 1930 to 1960 period, it was evident that no single monograph could encompass all the details of a whole "way of life" or "mode of thought" and that those were not as homogeneous and unitary as had been assumed. In a period when new nations were being built and when the subdivision and interdigitation of language groups had become very apparent, the question arose to what extent "tribes" were categories of colonial administration rather than sociologically definable units of analysis. Consequently, the problem of identifying meaningful boundaries of social fields when all social fields were penetrable was a serious one. The "tribe" did not constitute an adequate answer to such questions. The idea of the "tribe" was firmly fixed in the consciousness of Africans and outsiders, but it was far from a "natural" unit of analysis. It was patently not "natural," and for many issues did not represent the most meaningful unit of study.

An ever-fuller recognition of the complexity of social life, with its many varied situations, and an ever-growing acknowledgment of the multiplicity of ways in which the human existential predicament might be addressed competed in anthropology with the social scientists' will to generalize. Less and less could ethnographers conceive the fieldwork task as one of easily describing a sociocultural totality. "Tradition" became less and less the central focus. The fieldwork method demanded straight reportage of what happened at the time of observation at the site. One could not assume without close investigation that the next village in the area replicated the one under study.

Even during the colonial period, many writings went far to include what was visibly variable and notably changing in Africa (see, for example, Gluckman 1940, 1941, 1942, 1949; Wilson and Wilson 1968; Read 1938; Fortes 1936; Firth 1947; Forde 1937, 1939; Hunter 1936; Richards 1955; Schapera 1947; Gulliver 1955b, 1958). By the postcolonial period, "change" became the dominant preoccupation, just as "custom" had once been. Much that had once been seen as "custom" was reinterpreted as an artifact of a particular historical period, perhaps locally legitimated by being connected with the "traditional" but not necessarily having great historical depth in its current form.

The postcolonial wave of ethnography, even in its monographic form, has gone far beyond an earlier dehistoricized interest in Africa. The wave has entered intellectual territory in which the history of the colonial and postcolonial experience of any people and their contacts with central governments, with other peoples in Africa's generally plural societies, and with a transforming political economy weigh in heavily. Elements of local cultural distinctiveness remain of interest but only as these fit into a more complex and historically specific series of sequential pictures. This shift of focus in anthropology did not occur suddenly or abruptly. The groundwork was laid during the colonial period in the many studies not confined simply to folk traditions. In the post-colonial period, however, in anglophone Africanist studies at least, one of what had been two parallel tracks of earlier monographic production— the "traditions of" and the "current situation of" particular populations— gradually became one track in the new literature. The exclusively "traditions of" monograph was over as a major anthropological art form.

As Keith Hart said of the 1960s in his 1985 review of the social anthropology of West Africa,

It is a truism to say that decolonization transformed West African anthropology. Apart from anything else, it was hard to sustain a synchronic, local level approach to societies whose wholesale reconstruction was so visible, month to month. . . . Africa was the repository of unrealistic hopes for a better political and economic order. This was the decade of modernization, an American theory of social improvement. . . . Anthropologists made an explicit attempt at this time to break new ground, addressing economic development, pre-colonial history, urbanization, the position of women, and belief systems. None of this, as we have seen, is without precedent in the colonial literature. (249–50)

This last point also appears in Werbner's 1984 survey article on the Manchester school in south-central Africa, in which he illustrates the thematic foundations established during the colonial period that later became the point of departure for much subsequent work.

Yet some Africanist anthropology of the postcolonial period continued to use the classical strategy of explaining coherent "systems." Two approaches to system stood out in the 1960s and 1970s, one directed toward interpreting the internally consistent logics of religion, symbolic order, and modes of thought, and the other addressing the internal connections among politics, economy, and organization. But these, although "system" oriented, were addressed in new ways. French anthropology became the site of major innovative publications on those two themes, the structuralist and the neo-Marxist. The work of Claude Lévi-Strauss in structuralist theory had a tremendous impact on African studies, although his own field experience did not take place in Africa. Lévi-Strauss basically contended that all human beings have a powerful desire to understand the world as having an underlying logic, to make some kind of intellectual order out of the otherwise inexplicable jumble of elements in the social and physical environment. He contended that certain simple, universal principles of classification (or thought) were used to achieve this symbolic ordering of the materials of experience (1966). Because Lévi-Strauss focused entirely on discerning symbolic patternings and the significance that could be inferred from them, his work does not address actual behavior and thus does not tie the level of the symbolic to the level of action. Structuralism provided new, systematic ways of understanding the symbolic elements in culture, whether kinship terminologies, prescribed systems of marriage, or the symbols used in myth, ritual, and religion. Structuralism proposed a scheme for seeing what had previously appeared to be arbitrary and even fortuitous symbolic elements as elements in highly systematized representations of order in the cultural universe. This framework was easily and widely imitated.

Parallel to this development were the initiatives of the French neo-Marxists, which will be addressed in greater detail in the next section. A great wave of Marxist revisionism was then occupying the French intellectual community. This had considerable resonance among African intellectuals, many of whom were engaged in trying to build socialist principles into the structure of the new African nations. For decades there has been an intense francophone African dialogic contact with Parisian circles. The underlying reasons for the appeal of Marxist ideas were probably different for the two communities, one lodged in French postwar political history, the other in the African experience of gaining independence. In anthropology the French Marxists combined accounts of "primitive" material production with a fascination with its ideological rationalization. They asked new questions about the applicability of Marxist doctrine to "precapitalist" society. It is ironic, given the objections put forward by Mudimbe to "primitivist anthropology," that the idea of "the primitive" was pivotal particularly for certain structuralists and Marxists and that many of them were determinedly synchronic in their approach. Others, both Marxists and non-Marxists, were much more occupied with the analysis of the visible, contemporaneous Africa and the questions posed by its ongoing transformation.

The relationships among indigenous subsistence systems, trade, migrant labor, and other aspects of the world economy were urgent practical issues as well as matters of wide analytical interest. Thus, in addition to Marxist theoretical interests in these topics, there were parallel, non-Marxist studies of rural economies, rural entrepreneurs, and the division of labor in local communities and households. Many studies of economic development, planned and spontaneous, appeared and no doubt will continue to do so. Related to this, too, were studies of the African response to disasters arising from famines to political persecution.

The great importance of constructed gender differences and historical shifts in the relative positions of men and women also came to be the focus of a great deal of attention. Kinship studies continued but more dynamically than ever. Kinship was no longer seen as a set of practices that followed simply from a cluster of normative rules in the structural-functional manner. Instead, kinship was reinterpreted as a social resource usable for multiple economic, political, and reproductive ends, a set of cultural forms that could accommodate an immense variety of transformations. These are often visible in monographs on economic change.

The sixties also saw the beginnings of what has become a vigorous current discourse on the political relation between local communities and the developing forms of nationalism and the state. A number of works on the theme of cultural pluralism within nations were published during those years. It is not surprising that the concern about larger-than-local political organization and supra-local cultural and social structures should emerge as African states formed their postcolonial characters. An entirely new way of looking at African law also emerged. The earlier dichotomous model, dividing "customary" law from colonial law, was replaced by a historically informed conception. So-called "customary" systems were seen as arrangements radically remolded and redefined by colonial governments. Local systems of African law were recognized as continuously self-transforming and often forcibly transformed rather than representing a fixed "tradition," despite their being labeled as "customary."

This revised view of custom and the "traditional," has also permeated many other specialized subfields. It has become clear that what are culturally indubitably African creations are not necessarily historically old. Religion and "modes of thought" constitute another domain to which these considerations are pertinent. Unlike earlier versions of African religion, the newer works are as apt to deal with the way religious ideas have served as collective cultural and political responses to colonial and postcolonial pressures as they are to address the particular meanings internal to a system of ideas, symbols, and rituals. Medical anthropology combines the "systems of thought" perspective with practical interests and often overlaps the religious. Questions that surround modes of healing and the sense of well-being— social, psychological, and physical— have given major insights into systems of meaning.

Some contemporary approaches to the problems of meaning, of knowledge, of metaphor, of symbol, ask the kind of epistemological questions that appear in the current critique of anthropology. Michael Jackson has said, "Construing anthropology as *either* science *or* art, fact *or* fiction, true *or* false, knowledge *or* opinion, implies an absurd antinomy between objectivity and subjectivity, and the idea that we must somehow choose between one or the other. . . . The discourse of anthropology is a curious blend of both sorcery and science. . . . Let us then accept that there is no ahistorical, absolute, nonfinite reality *either outside or within us* that we can reach by adopting a particular discursive style. The *world* is out there, to be sure, and deep within us too, *but not the truth* (Rorty 1986, 3)" (Jackson 1989, 182). Using this kind of reasoning results in an intensely personal reading of the ethnographic evidence. There have been some experimental ethnographies of this genre in the Africanist field, some highly self-conscious attempts to decenter the fieldwork experience, to be open to acknowledging both the subjectivity of others and the presence of one's own self, to present one's own doubts and uncertainties as well as insights, also to acknowledge all the senses. These represent attempts to rethink the way ethnographic information is collected, to treat ethnography as an experience of mutuality rather than as a set of objectifying observations, to open all anthropologists' senses to what surrounds them, and to present what has been experienced in a reflexive way. The works that ask questions about the nature of knowledge are not only concerned to understand Africa and Africans but also to redefine anthropology.

All in all, this recent intellectual ferment has obviously responded to three decades of change in Africa and in the rest of the world and to concurrent changes in academe. There have been numerous shifts in perspective, but the new work nevertheless has strong links to earlier ethnographic efforts. A cumulative body of knowledge exists such that restudies and comparisons now permit diachronic and processual commentaries that were never possible in an earlier time. They would not be possible at all had the earlier work not been done. In addition, the changes that these historical and processual works trace could not have been easily accommodated in the accounts of cultural types with which the earlier compilers occupied themselves. New compendia seem to be being produced in two forms, either as articles on the state of the art in a particular subtopic of anthropology or on a particular theoretical school (see, for example, Guyer 1981 on household and community; Shipton 1990 on famines; Fernandez 1978 on religious movements; MacGaffey 1981 on ideology and belief; Sanjek 1990b on urban anthropology; Kahn and Llobera 1980 on Marxism) or in the form of encyclopedias. At least two are in progress at present, a general one edited by John Middleton and another on African religion under the editorship of V. Y. Mudimbe. The encyclopedia approach reflects the vastness of the body of knowledge that has now accumulated. The following brief review of the voluminous anthropological literature produced since midcentury represents just one segment of that information culled from one discipline. Even in that single field, the degree of diversity of topical focus that African studies now encompasses is evident.

Topics and Categories

Balandier and the French Marxists

Except for the long Dogon project of the Griaule school in France and the occasional Herskovits student in the United States, the almost exclusive dominance of British social anthropology in Africanist studies lasted well into the 1950s, when more French and American anthropologists began to appear on the scene. In France there is no doubt that the turning point was the influence of Georges Balandier, himself well acquainted with and profoundly influenced by his British predecessors and contemporaries. As Claude Meillassoux said in a 1981 tribute in which he referred to his first fieldwork in 1957 under Balandier's direction, "Balandier introduced me to the best of current anthropology— that is to British anthropology— which provided me with some of the best research on this topic. . . . Balandier was not only a researcher and a teacher, he was also the promoter of African studies in France. Most French Africanists today owe their careers to him, even those who now work in different schools of thought" (Meillassoux 1981, vii, viii, ix; see also Adler et al. 1986).

In 1954 Balandier organized a program of study, the "Sociologie de l'Afrique Noire" in section 6 of the Ecole des Hautes Etudes of the Sorbonne, to which other programs were later added. These programs of teaching and research constituted the nucleus of the Centre d'Études Africaines, established in 1957. Balandier also founded and became director of the African studies section of the Fondation des Sciences Politiques (Paris) in 1959 to undertake the study of African political parties, doctrines, and ideologies (Balandier 1960). He also served as the director of the International Research Office on Social Implications of Technological Change and was a member of the executive council of the International African Institute. These institution-building activities were of great importance in going beyond the earlier, Griaule-inspired, French tradition of study, which had been preoccupied with indigenous African thought and philosophy. Balandier's earlier books, *Sociologie des Brazzavilles noires* (1955), *Sociologie actuelle de l'Afrique noire* (1955), and *Afrique ambiguë* (1957), marked a major change in perspective. They directly addressed the varieties of modern African communities and how these had come into being. The Brazzavilles book concerned urban life, the first such study by a sociologist-anthropologist in francophone Africa. This innovative urban research was produced at roughly the same time as that of the various Rhodes-Livingstone Manchester school studies of the towns of the copper belt in what was then Northern Rhodesia (Epstein 1958; Mitchell 1956).

All of these midcentury books centered on the history as well as the economic and demographic transformations that African societies had undergone. Balandier interpreted new religious movements as political reactions to colonial power and raised questions about the then current attitudes of the decolonizing period. In *Sociologie Actuelle,* he specifically compared the histories of the Fang and the Ba-Kongo and their reactions to the colonial situation. This was not fieldwork in the manner of Malinowski or of the British school. These were not detailed descriptions of day-to-day life or of the interactions of individuals, although Balandier had interviewed many persons, had been in the field, and gave substantial attention to the structures of kinship. Nevertheless, the material presented was organized as a historical and sociological overview that relied heavily on reinterpreting administrative records, censuses, and other archival materials as well as on statistical data produced through surveys and questionnaires. The historical argument carried forward a documented description of the effects on particular African peoples of imposed changes and of the reaction to the shocks of the colonial period. This was a major change of path. It was an ambitious attempt to "élucider la relation entre phénomènes sociaux totaux et dynamique sociale totale" (Balandier 1963, 503).

In a candid autobiographical reminiscence (1977), Balandier spoke not only of his reaction to his various postings, travels, and research periods in Africa but also about some of the persons he met and befriended. Balandier makes evident the difference between his situation in Africa and that of later anthropologists who worked in the postcolonial era. Balandier, attuned to the impending changes and sympathetic to the African impatience for independence, came to know many African intellectuals in his first decades of work. Many of the persons to whom he had easy access in those years subsequently became major political figures in the new Africa. He clearly had contact with an Africa that was on the move, and that was the way he conceived and wrote about it.

The changes in temporal and analytic perspective initiated by Balandier were infused with a high degree of political awareness. Indeed, Balandier's short, general, text-like essay, *Political Anthropology* (1970), became a minor classic. This independent line of political, economic, and cultural study was followed by Balandier and his students at the very time that Lévi-Straussian structuralism reached its height in France and abroad.

In a recently published volume of tribute to Balandier by his students, Terray explains that the whole cohort that studied with him in the 1960s came to work with Balandier only after having carefully studied the works of the Griaule school and after being seduced by the intellectuality and logic of Lévi-Strauss, all the while knowing that this work was in another world from that of the oppressed and rebellious third world of the time when Patrice Lumumba and Che Guevara walked (Terray 1986, 10). Then they discovered Balandier, who introduced them to the Africa he knew, an Africa replete with conflict, a dynamic Africa in which Africans strategized to survive amid the crises they experienced and constructed new forms. Balandier also introduced them to the classics of the British school, emphasizing particularly the works of Max Gluckman, whose theoretical approach Balandier and his students found appealing and closest to Balandier's own approach.

From the 1960s on a substantial recasting and harnessing of the Balandier models to the purposes of a Marxist anthropology occurred. A Marxist approach to economic anthropology was becoming a major force in the discipline in general, with

Maurice Godelier as one of the major proponents. As Copans (1977) put it, Balandier's approach was close enough to Marxism for the transition from "a dynamic to a Marxist explanation to be made by filiation and not by rupture" (25). Many of the Africanists became actively engaged in this theoretical discourse. Of Balandier's students, Claude Meillassoux stands as an early and influential example of what became of the Marxist themes when applied to the history of particular African peoples.

Meillassoux's study of the Gouro (1964a) follows the Balandier pattern but injects a new preoccupation, the theoretical question of whether Marxist models could be effectively applied to so-called precapitalist societies and cultures. By implication, he further posed the question of whether Marxist models themselves could be revised and refined in the light of such an application. In the Gouro project, Meillassoux combined intermittent periods of fieldwork in the Ivory Coast with investigations of the archives to reconstruct a picture of a precolonial system and its subsequent transformation. The ethnography he eventually produced gives little sense of that immediacy of contact with Africans and the lively and specific instances of strategies used in managing a mundane daily life that are regularly found in accounts produced in the British school. The temporal choices made by Meillassoux may have made that impossible. After all, his fieldwork was not contemporaneous with either of the historical periods with which he was theoretically most concerned, the precolonial and the early and middle colonial. The seminal idea that Meillassoux generated from the Gouro material and wanted to extend to other social types was an abstract model of a self-sustaining precapitalist society (1960, 1964a, 1964b, 1968a, 1984). Meillassoux's work and that of other French Marxists often combined two quite different interests, an evolutionist's fascination with timeless self-reproducing primitive "types," and a passionate political preoccupation with the transformations worked by colonial domination and capitalist penetration.

The French Marxists by no means agreed with one another,

either on all points of anthropological theory or on matters of French and African politics. (For a very useful summary of the issues and personalities of the period, see Kahn and Llobera 1980; see also Bloch 1984). Though they could all be characterized as major participants in the Marxist discourse from the 1960s to the present, Emmanuel Terray, Georges Dupré, Pierre Philippe Rey, Jean Copans, and Marc Augé have all approached African studies and anthropology itself from quite different perspectives. Terray did his thesis fieldwork among the Dida of the Ivory Coast, and he produced his book about the Dida (1969b) within Balandier's conceptual framework. Terray's theoretical work took another turn, however. His *Le Marxisme devant les sociétés primitives* (1969a) attempted to apply the formulations of Louis Althusser to a rereading of Lewis Henry Morgan and to serve as the basis for yet another reconstruction of Gouro society. Terray then turned his hand to a further reconstruction, this time that of the history of the Abron kingdom of Guyaman (1974). These works had much more to do with the then ongoing Marxist professional dialogue in Paris than they did with the contemporary realities of life in Africa.

On an entirely different track are Rey's books and papers, which concern colonialism, neocolonialism, the development of capitalism and class formation, particularly in Congo-Brazzaville (1969, 1971, 1973, 1975; see also Dupré and Rey 1969). Rey, too, had participated in the purely theoretical arguments of the late 1960s. In that heady period, very much influenced by Althusser, Rey and Dupré collaborated to produce an influential article proposing a theory of exchange (1969; see more recently Parry and Bloch 1989). After Coquery-Vidrovitch's attempt to identify a specifically "African mode of production" (1969) Rey also published on the lineage mode of production, a concept that has been perceptively criticized by Guyer (Rey 1969, 1975; Guyer 1981). Of this group of Balandier's Marxist students, perhaps the most durably and currently influential has been Marc Augé. His Africanist work has followed a very different route, much more concerned with symbol, thought, and ideology (1969, 1975, 1977). Augé's purely theoretical book, *Symbole, fonction, histoire* (1979), provides a glimpse of the extent to which he considers works of the British school fundamental to a general definition of the anthropological project. The influence of Balandier is unmistakable.

Economy, Kinship, and Gender

Many post–1960s publications focused on local economies. They built on earlier studies, such as those of Richards on land, labor, and diet (1939); Forde and Scott on the native economies of Nigeria (1946); Bohannan on farming, exchange, investment, and the impact of money (1954, 1955, 1959); Gulliver on the property of pastoralists, labor migration, and land tenure (1955a, 1955b, 1958); and M. G. Smith on Hausa economy (1955). The writing that followed (and some of the older monographs as well) emphasized transformations, variations, and economic differentiation. The foundational work on kinship had prepared the way for the domestic domain and its economy to come into the limelight as a distinct field of study. An argument not unlike that of Chayanov (which was not widely known among English speakers until it was translated, years later, in 1966) was incorporated into anthropological thought in 1958 with the publication of Jack Goody's *The Developmental Cycle in Domestic Groups*. The fact that the labor available to a household expands and contracts at various points in the history of a family and that the number of economically unproductive dependents also varies over time destroyed once and for all the notion that the family could be thought of as having a single form in any society. Variability was not only normal but inevitable, and it had distinct economic consequences. This amending of the classic structural model of kinship shifted the center of theoretical discussion from norms to practices, from culture to demography, from standardization to variation, from structure to process.

As is evident, Goody branched off from Meyer Fortes's tradition, still preoccupied with kinship but in a materialist yet non-Marxist direction. Goody's had enormous and continuous influence in anthropology, both before and after he succeeded Fortes in the chair at Cambridge. Goody published indefatigably on subjects ranging from kinship to studies of cooking and class, from state formation to mythology (1958, 1961, 1962, 1967, 1968, 1969, 1971, 1972, 1973, 1976, 1977, 1979, 1982, 1986a, 1986b, 1990a, 1990b, 1992). Goody's interest in kinship had a distinctly property-oriented cast from the beginning, as is evident from his early monograph, *Death, Property, and the Ancestors* (1962). His preoccupation with the relationship between kinship organization and the control of property later reemerged in his large-scale comparison between Africa and Europe, *Production and Reproduction: A Comparative Study of the Domestic Domain* (1976). Goody built his argument on the difference between marriage and inheritance in societies in which class was a major structural feature (Europe and Asia) and societies in which it was not (Africa). It was a statistically grounded effort to identify related clusters of variables surrounding radically different family systems (see also Goody and Tambiah 1973). Interest in the bridewealth question has continued, as demonstrated by John Comaroff's edited volume, *The Meaning of Marriage Payments* (1980), and Adam Kuper's *Wives for Cattle* (1982) (see also Guyer 1986, 1988; Parkin and Nyamwaya 1987).

Study of the domestic economy leads quickly to the gender-marked division of labor in Africa and, indeed, to the whole question of the construction of gender and the control of marriage in African society (Guyer 1986). It is no accident that two of Meillassoux's major books concerned the relationship among marriage, kinship, and property in precapitalist and capitalist circumstances. He described (1964a) in striking way the relationship between economic production and reproduction, the manner in which male elders once controlled the labor of juniors through the manipulation of bridewealth payments and the timing of marriage. He restates the theoretical argument in much more general terms, particularly in relation to modern labor migration, in *Maidens, Meal, and Money* (1984).

There now is a growing literature on the subject of the gendered division of labor and on other aspects of the situation of African women. The quality of the data collected has changed considerably, as has the perspective. Examples of this phenomenon include Kaberry 1952; Paulme 1960; Obbo 1975, 1980; Wilson 1977; Bledsoe 1980; Étienne and Leacock 1980; Oppong 1983; Swantz 1985; Little 1973; LeVine 1979; Bay 1982; Guyer 1984a, 1988, 1991. This topic is one on which the last word has surely not been said.

Guyer's "Household and Community in African Studies" (1981) provides an excellent introduction to the literature on households. Guyer's own fieldwork (1980, 1984b), informed by attention to the gender question, combines a meticulous attention to ethnographic detail with the posing of important theoretical questions. In one comparative paper (1984b), she addressed critically the assertion that root crops are "women's crops" because they are "naturally" better fitted to women's domestic duties than grains as there is considerable choice about the timing of root-crop harvesting and much less leeway for grains. Guyer answers by shifting to a different question, showing instead the relevance and importance of the social capacity to mobilize collective labor for the harvesting of grain crops, a capacity that women are regularly denied in many African societies. The two questions— what kind of return do women get for their labor and what sorts of choices are open to women as they negotiate their positions in the world— will surely continue to be addressed in the African context as elsewhere (see Guyer 1991). In Africa, however, these issues may be raised with greater urgency because the situation of many African women is worsening, yet their role in a faltering system of production remains critical.

A major work of the 1960s, the Polanyi-inspired collection of papers on African markets edited by Bohannan and Dalton (1962; see also Meillassoux 1971), drew the attention of economic anthropologists in a very different direction. This was followed a few years later by Paul and Laura Bohannan's *Tiv Economy* (1968), which built on Paul Bohannan's earlier general ethnography (1953). The perception of marketing issues was considerably expanded by Cohen's excellent study of Hausa traders in Ibadan (1969). Trading diasporas had long been central to the regional economy of West Africa, but as long as anthropologists confined themselves to studying "tribes" and small local communities as isolates, the cultural implications of these networks of long-distance exchange did not receive adequate attention. Cohen's work not only contributed to an understanding of the extensive geographical reach of ethnic trading monopolies in West Africa, but it showed the links among ethnicity, religion, and economy. The book addressed the idea of "tribal" identity as a construct, noting the existence of "retribalization," the building and hardening of new versions of ethnic boundaries. The passage of time formed an important part of his analysis. Cohen showed that the development of new Islamic religious practices and consequently of new forms of ethnic distinctiveness had both political and economic consequences for the Hausa. The analytic boundaries between conventionally conceived institutional systems— economy, religion, and politics— were once again broken down by attention to a new cluster of ethnographic facts.

Polly Hill's book on migrant cocoa farmers in Ghana (1963) broke further new ground in describing lively African entrepreneurial activity and its social concomitants. Her later work in northern Nigeria (1977) sketched a historical sequence of economic transformation among the Hausa, and by the mid–1980s Hill was ready for an all-out attack on development economics (1986). This sequence in her work represents a widespread set of attitudes in Africanist economic anthropology in the decades after independence. There existed a fascination with ongoing African economic activity and the social relations surrounding it, a growing preoccupation with economic history in Africa, and dismay over many development policies of governments and international agencies.

The questions addressed were broadened. On a historical theme that also had vast regional implications, several anthropologists edited books on the history of slavery (Meillassoux 1975; Miers and Kopytoff 1977). Anthropology expanded its problematic. Keith Hart wrote an overview of the rise of commercial farming in West Africa and its impact on the communities of the area (1982). Colin Murray's 1981 book on the disrupting effects of migrant labor on family life in southern Africa set a very high standard of evidentiary documentation and empathy. D. Cruise O'Brien depicted the close connections among colonial policy, the rise of the Islamic Mourides brotherhoods in Senegal, and the related spread and development of peanut farming (1975). In East Africa, Parkin addressed the consequences of the expansion of the palm wine business in a succinct and persuasive account (1972). The theme of transformation, often with economic underpinnings, came to dominate the literature (Colson 1971; Karp 1978; Vincent 1982; Moore 1986; Parkin and Nyamwaya 1987; Colson and Scudder 1975, 1988; Pottier 1988; Jules-Rosette 1981; Linares 1992). There seems little doubt, too, that rural studies were in this respect affected by anthropological inquiries into the patterns of growing inequality and ethnic separatism in the urban areas (Little 1973; Lloyd 1974; Parkin 1978; see also Coquery-Vidrovitch 1988, 1991 and the discussion of urban studies above).

A recent highly varied set of writings illustrates the current degree of specialized attention to urgent practical issues in anthropological approaches to African economic life, for example, Pottier's edited volume, *Food Systems in Central and Southern Africa* (1985), and Shipton's bibliographical survey of the literature on African famines (1990) (see also Shipton 1988, 1989). The far-reaching consequences of chronic food shortage are plainly very much a part of the present in Africa. The most extreme disasters have caused many deaths, but the survivors of the less drastic shortages have had to draw on all they know of lifesaving strategies and culturally structured protective responses to remain alive. Drawn together, the story is one of suffering, of ingenuity, and sometimes of heroic courage. The details are factually and analytically important, because the topical comparative survey adds a generalizing dimension to the classical preoccupation with community study in ethnography.

Along similar methodological lines, Robertson (1987) has made a comparative survey of share contracts all over Africa, showing how widespread and how much of a creative resource this strategy of production can be and how remarkably varied in its local details. A gloomier work, Downs and Reyna (1988), addresses the social and political factors surrounding land tenure in eleven localities. This collection emphasizes restrictions on access, growing insecurity of tenure, increasing economic differentiation, and the failure of many policies of land-tenure reform. Demonstrating that land-reform measures in Kenya have increased rather than decreased rural inequality, Riley and Brokensha, a geographer and an anthropologist, add their voices to an increasing number of skeptical assessments of development policies (1988) (see also Horowitz and Painter 1986 and Shipton 1988).

These recent products of postcolonial economic anthropology show how the discipline itself has been affected by the changing economic circumstances of rural and urban Africans. A strong "social problem" component is visible, but prescriptions and solutions are in short supply. The Marxist tradition continues in new forms (see, for example, Donham 1990). Whereas many recent works on economy concern the way particular Africans make a living and strategize about doing so, they are also in varying degrees given to setting those activities within large-scale social, political, and historical frameworks (see Linares 1992). They simultaneously ask questions about the subjects' conceptions, intentions, and ideologies. The location of "culture" in these discussions varies and by implication raises the question of whether culture remains the all-purpose analytical concept it once seemed to be.

French Structuralism and Other Approaches to Modes
of Thought, Religion, and the Symbolic Order

Social anthropology since the 1960s also experienced a renaissance of interest in religion, ritual, and other symbolic forms. John Middleton's 1960 study, *Lugbara Religion,* presented a detailed case study of the political struggles imbedded in the ritual life of one village of a northern Uganda people. The book rapidly became a classic, fitting as it did within the tendency of the British school to see ritual as a recorded expression of social relations. Turner (1957) had constructed the framework, but Middleton developed it further with a less harmonious interpretation. Fortes and Dieterlen gave the topic of religion and cosmological ideas a further boost by together editing an influential book, *African Systems of Thought* (1965). At around the same time, the structuralism of Lévi-Strauss crossed the channel and became a prominent theme in some British symbolic interpretations, although it never enjoyed the same dominance it had in French writings. The British school never suspended its interest in politics and economy. In its "pure" form, the Lévi-Straussian focus on the order in symbolic systems and the regularities of combination, opposition, and parallelism to be found among the symbolic elements was emphatically nonsociological, noneconomic, and nonpolitical. There were many Africanists, even among those who were did not see his approach as the only acceptable one, who found and continued to find in the question of classification an illuminating approach to African cosmologies, rituals, myths, and other symbolic inventions (DeHeusch 1958, 1972, 1985; Douglas 1966; Willis 1974; Bourdieu 1977; Barley 1983). MacGaffey's "African Ideology and Belief" offers a useful general survey of writings on African ideology and belief, not only anthropological and structuralist, also including Islam and Christianity as well as indigenous systems (see also Fernandez 1978, 1979, 1982; Beidelman 1974, 1982, 1986).

For structuralists, the structuralist method revealed a hidden or submerged grammar-like order in symbolic systems. Critics of structuralism saw the method itself as producing rather than uncovering the orderliness it "discovered" (Goody 1961, 1972, 1977; Moore 1976). And others "explained" African religions or symbolic systems with other rationales, as modes of reasoning that could be likened to Western scientific speculation (Horton 1967, 1971, 1975) or as comprehensible in terms of the unconscious meanings they expressed, which, it was argued, could be recovered through psychoanalytic interpretation (Beidelman 1968), as organizing metaphors (Fernandez 1974), or as modes of protest (Bourdillon 1971; Comaroff 1985).

Others joined the debate about meaning from other angles, for example considering the differences in perspective between insider and outsider and dealing with religion as a performative presentation (Harris 1978) or attacking the idea that there are underlying meanings in symbols that can be discerned by semiologists and anthropologists and arguing instead that these are insertions of the observer's views (Sperber 1974; for a diverse range of interpretations of African thought and symbol, see also Richards 1967; Beattie and Middleton 1969; Karp and Bird 1980; Thornton 1980; Beidelman 1968, 1986; James 1988).

Medical anthropology offers another locus for the discussion of symbolic constructs, one illuminated by its practical and applied context (Feierman 1979; Augé and Herzlich 1984; Mullings 1984; Buckley 1985; Sargent 1989). Histories of African medicine often draw on anthropological perspectives; thus, a recent set of essays in the tradition of Foucault (Vaughan 1991) addresses the European colonial discourse on African illness. This work uses archival materials on the symbols and practices of biomedicine as an access route to the colonial imagination.

As one might expect, quite a different vision of the significance of symbol and ritual is found in the various Marxist interpretations (Binsbergen 1981; Binsbergen and Schoffeleers 1985). Thus, one classic version put forward by the politically minded emphasizes that ritual communication concerns and furthers the interests of dominant groups (Bloch 1984). To a different effect is an interpretation of religion as the expression of a particular mode of production (Rigby 1981; Augé 1975). Outside the Marxist tradition others also contend that ritual and symbol at the very least serve "to inculcate respect for tradition and hierarchy" as MacGaffey characterizes LaFontaine's position (1981, 253; LaFontaine 1977, 1985; see also Kopytoff 1971, 1981, on ancestors and elders, and Parkin 1991 on spatial images that reflect history).

Within another stream of research, many recent works have addressed the rapidly expanding Islamic and Christian influences in Africa and their local variations of experience, practice, and thought (Comaroff and Comaroff 1991; Holy 1991). The first volume of the Comaroffs' history concerns itself with early missionary contacts, with, as they put it, "the colonization of consciousness and the consciousness of colonization." Holy addresses the intertwining of Islam and local "custom" in a gendered form. He argues that among the Berti, Islamic practice is primarily conceived of as male, whereas local, non-Islamic practices are very much in the female domain. The preoccupation of the Comaroffs and of Holy with the nature of consciousness, with the contents of the imagination, with the cultural aspects of domination, both in the setting of the colonial period and in the gender politics of the present, is in keeping with significant contemporary currents in anthropological thought.

The process of acceptance or rejection of the proselytizing world religions has become part of another problematic: the interest in multilevel analysis. A rich literature has grown up around local cults and the alternative versions of world religions devised by Africans. Significant works include studies of missionizing, of conversion, of the political significance of regional cults, and— perhaps most important of all— of the characteristics of the indigenized churches, of ethnic and class religious practice, and of the self-conscious symbolic intent of some of the new religions of Africa (Fernandez 1978, 1979, 1982; Beattie and Middleton 1969; Horton 1971, 1975; Beidelman 1974, 1982, 1986; Lewis 1966; Jules-Rosette 1975; Cohen 1969, 1981; Comaroff 1985; Peel 1968, 1977; MacGaffey 1981, 1983; Werbner 1977; Daneel 1971, 1974; Murphee 1969).

There have also been some tantalizing experiments with building ethnographic narratives out of intimate accounts of the fieldwork experience (Riesman 1977; Stoller 1986, 1987; Jackson 1977, 1989). Its proponents conceive of this genre as a major break with the past. The presentation emphasizes that the anthropologist is an actor in the fieldwork scene, an active presence that must be accounted for. The dialogic content of contacts are strongly acknowledged, as is the subjectivity of both the anthropologist and the persons with whom he/she interacts. This format tends to enlarge on particular incidents and to present detailed sketches of individuals in the midst of the encounter with the anthropologist. People are heard and seen doing things in their lives, alluding to their life stories, recounting their dilemmas, presenting their opinions as individuals, and explaining their actions and those of others. This type of ethnography about particular persons rejects the idea of abstracting a generalized, supposedly objectified version of "the culture" and/or "the society." These anthropologists argue that insight comes through the effort to understand particular interchanges with individuals, to apprehend the way others conceive of themselves in relation to the anthropologist, to learn how they think about their affairs and manage their lives. Of course, this managing of individual lives takes place within a larger cultural and social milieu that is of more than passing professional interest. This viewpoint holds, however, that only through specific personalities and their own reflections on their lives can that meaning of the milieu be understood.

For all their subtlety, candor, humaneness, and verisimilitude, there is a cost to these transference-like approaches to the subjectivities of others in which anthropologists try to surrender themselves to the inner reality of others' lives. Accounts of these encounters are preoccupied with self, with the anthropologist's self and the selves of the anthropologist's interlocutors. Of necessity, therefore, these studies focus so much on the immediately present, on the microscale, on imagining the meanings of individual communications, and on detail that the larger-scale social context often disappears from view. The proponents of this kind of intersubjectivity accuse more conventional ethnographers of selective distortions of perception and presentation, and they are right. Yet this intensely experiential approach has its own distortions, however attractive and moving the narratives. To concentrate on what others are thinking and imagining, to focus on the way they see the world by trying to see it their way, is to ask a particular set of questions about the raw materials of thought. But other questions remain to be asked. In other approaches a less interior, more public social world is given primacy and the conventional explanatory discourse used in that social world is one of the primary objects analyzed. To be concerned with standardized forms of cultural discourse is not to deny the singularity of individual intentions and understandings. Individuals always give terms their own glosses and use them to their own purposes. There is no escape from selectivity and interpretation whatever anthropological route to meanings is chosen.

Politics, Pluralism, and Law

Most topics in Africanist anthropology necessarily have political dimensions; thus, much political observation is folded into small-scale ethnographic studies that focus on economy, kinship, ethnicity, religion, and the like. Such works tend to describe local micropolitics. Far fewer books and papers have much to say about the national scale, how its existence is experienced locally, let alone how the political level of supranational activity penetrates local life (for works that do address this subject, see Geschiere 1982; Binsbergen 1992). One anthropological approach much in favor at the moment is to ask the question of how individual and collective identity are constructed and used. This way of putting the matter necessarily implies attending to both local and large-scale issues. The reframing of questions about cultural politics in terms of "identity" has responded both to the intensive politicization of ethnic difference in many parts of the world today and to a growing interest in individual experience.

The emerging "identity" framework represents a substantial departure from the preoccupations of the classical period of Africanist political anthropology. Much of the political anthropology in African studies at midcentury and even later was concerned with elaborating the two types set out earlier by Fortes and Evans-Pritchard (1940), when they contrasted acephalous systems with centralized systems and with a third type, the segmentary state introduced by Southall (1954, 1988).

This typologizing led to two major streams of work. One focused on acephalous organization and its varieties, with some intermediate and mixed types also noted (Gulliver 1955a; Smith 1956; Middleton and Tait 1958; Lewis 1961; Spencer 1965; Dyson-Hudson 1966; Stewart 1977; Baxter and Almagor 1978). The other stream concentrated on African rulers and African bureaucracy (Nadel 1942; Gluckman 1943a, 1943b; Kuper 1947; Colson and Gluckman 1951; Southall 1954, 1988; Fallers 1956, 1964; Schapera 1956; Mitchell 1956; Richards 1959; Smith 1960; Southwold 1960; Mair 1962; Buxton 1963; Middleton 1965; Ruel 1969; Beattie 1971). Weak kings and strong kings, princes and chiefs, village headmen, lineage leaders, hierarchy and equality, social order with and without rulers were the structural preoccupations of political anthropology. And then there also were monographs like Turner's (1957) and Middleton's (1960) that depicted the machinations of ambitious men at the micropolitical level, showing their strategies of competition. (For an excellent review of the ethnographic literature exposing a full range of these issues in a particular region, the Sudan and Ethiopia, see James 1990.)

Of course, with very few exceptions, the actual fieldwork observation of African politics and government during the pre-independence period involved studying African hierarchies operating under the aegis of colonial authorities. To the extent that some anthropologists conceived their task as confined to the analysis of the "purely" African side of the equation, such approaches often paid insufficient attention to the effects of the larger political environment. By no means was all ethnographic work limited in this way, however (see, for example, Forde 1939; Gluckman 1940, 1943a, 1949). With the end of colonial rule and, in many (though not all) countries, the rejection of African rulers perceived as colonial agents, a new era opened and another set of questions arose. As early as 1966 Peter Lloyd edited a volume, *The New Elites of Tropical Africa* (on elites, see also Cohen 1981; Oppong 1974; Scudder and Colson 1980).

In the first flush of independence and new nationhood, some anthropologists attempted to address the potential character of the new African states. Internal diversity was the issue. One perspective considered the central process of incorporating of local systems into national ones (as in Cohen and Middleton 1970). Another more pessimistic view examined the extent to which cultural pluralism in Africa had been hardened and officialized into a structurally "corporate" form (Mitchell 1960; Kuper and Smith 1969). The example of South Africa remained very much in the minds of these theorists of African pluralism. Their models covered the range from simple instances of politically unformalized cultural difference between groups within a state to those circumstances in which culturally distinct populations were constitutionally recognized as the official units of incorporation into the national polity and were the entities through which the rights of citizen-members were determined. In the colonial period, an overarching state, indirect rule, and "customary law" had a tendency to transform simple cultural difference into differential incorporation. Such incorporation was also an obvious phenomenon in the history of South Africa. In short, in postcolonial anthropology the analysis of the politics of cultural difference became part of the discipline as never before. Culture lost whatever political innocence it ever had.

The importance, moreover, of interethnic contacts— polyethnic communities, cults that stretch over multiethnic regions, and political, economic, and other interethnic interdependencies— began to receive increasing attention in anthropology (see Parkin 1990, commenting to this effect on the East African literature as pioneering works and citing Southall 1954, 1970; Rigby 1969; and Spencer 1973). Urban studies undoubtedly fed back into rural ones some of the emphases on complex multiethnic relationships (for example, Parkin 1975). There has been a growing tendency to rethink many African situations in this way and to question the utility of relying on the supposed ethnic isolate as the premise of analysis. The political importance of ethnic boundaries is clearly a circumstantial creation, not a "natural" accompaniment of cultural difference. On the other side of the puzzle, polyethnic connections are by no means of only one type. The increasingly sophisticated intertwining of politics, cultural issues, administrative policy, and individual strategies in analysis is manifest not only in theoretical work on pluralism but in many politically oriented studies of particular peoples (Colson 1971, 1976; Parkin 1975; Bond 1976; Karp 1978; Burnham 1980; Colson and Scudder 1988; Van Binsbergen and Geschiere 1985).

After the first postindependence wave of optimism, postcolonial anthropologists were for the most part silent on the subject of African national regimes. No doubt this was for practical professional considerations as well as for reasons imbedded in the discipline's localist methods. Silence about the national level was presumably motivated in part by the anthropologist's desire to be permitted to return to the country being studied. Anthropologists cannot diplomatically analyze topics that would lead them to criticize directly the very governments on whose permission they depend to carry forward their research projects. Also, on methodological grounds, the long tradition of local, small-scale studies to which anthropology has made such a signal contribution seems to conveniently justify silence about the large scale. Both of these circumstances have no doubt contributed to anthropological reticence about national politics.

Of course, no such inhibitions pertain to the colonial period, because it has ended. Consequently, the colonial era has represented an inviting field for retrospective analysis, particularly for certain topics on which there are ample records. Thus, for example, both Snyder and Moore have written ethnographic monographs that also trace century-long transformations of local forms of African law (Snyder 1981; Moore 1986). Both books follow the deep economic changes that underlay apparent manifestations of cultural continuity, Snyder in a Marxist mode, Moore in an eclectic vein. The idea of "customary law" would never be the same again, nor indeed, the idea of custom itself (see also Chanock 1985 and Mann and Roberts 1991).

The anthropological study of African law went through a series of additive and revisionist phases that led up to this recent processual, historico-ethnographic approach. The several perspectives developed sequentially but overlapped and only partly replaced each other. First came the long stream of attempts to set down customary law in the form of a set of rules that could guide judges (Schapera 1938; Holleman 1952; Allott 1969). This technique, initiated in the colonial period, continued for a time in the postcolonial states. Gluckman's ethnography (1955) introduced the quite different strategy of listening to litigation in a Lozi court and giving accounts of the facts of specific cases and such legal rules and principles as were enunciated in the decision-making process. Bohannan followed with a short book (1957) on Tiv hearings in and out of the formal court system, emphasizing indigenous key concepts as the path to understanding their legal thought. Gluckman (no doubt affected by the discussions generated by the Bohannan work) subsequently wrote a concepts book of his own about the guiding ideas and principles in Barotse law distilled from his earlier field experience (1965).

In the same period, Philip Gulliver's 1963 analysis of social control among a group of agricultural Maasai (the Arusha) introduced a new angle. He deemphasized "customary rules" and "concepts" as determinative of case outcomes and contended instead that in certain systems outcomes depended more on the political power of the winning litigant than on normative propositions (see also Heald 1989 on controlling violence). Comaroff and Roberts (1981) responded to this controversy over "rule orders" versus "power" by developing a complex picture of practice. They showed the contenders' perspective in great detail, describing the various strategies of argument deployed by litigants among the Tswana and the effects of these strategies on various phases of disputation. Snyder and Moore's studies differed from the others in that though they analyzed instances of litigation, they centered on the historical context within which disputes between individuals took place rather than concentrating exclusively on the disputing process.

Much ferment exists in anthropology today on the topic of African politics, what with the end of the cold war and the major transformations now underway from South Africa to North Africa. The pervasive issue of politicized cultural (ethnic?) differences has already manifested itself and will surely reshape some of Africa. The next few years will surely see a new anthropology of new African political situations. (For a recent general overview of the history of political anthropology by an Africanist, see Vincent 1990.)

Three recent works illustrate some of the strong topical and methodological shifts that are now visible and the great variety of approaches within the same topical field. The first, *Power, Prayer, and Production: The Jola of Senegal,* by Olga Linares (1992), succinctly illustrates the striking cultural diversity found among the five hundred or so Jola communities in Senegal. Linares does this by describing three different "regional social formations" epitomized by three communities in which she has done field work over a number of years. The three communities have had different historical experiences, one adopting Islam and commercial crops, one not having been Islamicized, and the third adopting various organizational and religious features of Manding culture. Linares uses their history to argue that the differences among them are "not simply the direct unproblematic consequence of the penetration of world market forces, or capitalist relations of production. . . . They are also a result of the often contradictory ways in which ideological processes have negotiated between old practices and new economic opportunities" (7). This is a rare attempt to achieve a kind of controlled comparison in narrative form. It grounds ethnography in history, paying simultaneous attention to material factors, to systems of belief, and to structures of organization. This complex overview illustrates a significant current in present-day Africanist anthropology, namely the tendency to give a substantial place to quite specific, historically informed analysis that does not simply attribute all change in the past century to a formulaic, universalizing interpretation of the colonial experience.

The second book is that by David Lan, *Guns and Rain* (1985), a monograph about modern guerilla warfare waged with the blessing (and practical help) of local spirit mediums in what is now northeastern Zimbabwe. The northeastern Shona about whom Lan writes live on both sides of the Mozambique-Zimbabwe border and crossed back and forth in the lengthy war to liberate Southern Rhodesia. The spirit mediums and chiefdoms of the area had been studied in an earlier period by Garbett (1966, 1969, 1977) and by Bourdillon (1979, 1981, 1982). Lan drew on their material and added his own data. The central feature of Lan's fieldwork was a set of interviews with veterans of the fighting and with the spirit mediums who helped them. Lan shows that the guerillas could never have achieved their purposes without the cooperation of the mediums, and he shows how it worked. He presents the extraordinary symbiosis, commonality of purpose, and syncretism of belief that developed between the mediums and the fighters during the war as well as some of the local political and historical background that fed into the construction of that extraordinary relationship.

The third study that illustrates changing foci in political anthropology is James Ferguson's *The Anti-Politics Machine* (1990), which describes in considerable detail the case history of a failed development project in Lesotho. The book gives an account of the sequence of events and also provides a commentary on how all those involved thought and talked about the project of development. It is not simply about what happened. The problematic interlock between the acknowledgment and denial of political realities forms the theoretical center of this extended case history. Many layers of meaning are addressed. The villagers depended economically on sending men to South Africa as migrant laborers, but the project and funding agencies sought to improve local agricultural and stock-raising practice, not directly to ameliorate the circumstances of labor migration over which they had neither jurisdiction nor control. Fieldwork among villagers showed how present-oriented was their "traditional" interest in cattle. Fieldwork among officials (and analysis of their documentary products) showed their quite different construction of the social environment in which they worked. Like Lan's book, this one draws on multisite study, on contacts with different people with different perspectives who are in contact with each other in the same milieu, trying together to bring about an explicitly predefined result.

The recent legal and political books mentioned here are studies built around topically strong themes. Accounts also exist of particular "peoples" of Africa. Distinctive local cultural practices are part of the story, but these books are most of all about a particular moment in history and what happened at that time in that setting. Theoretical questions are at issue, but they are not the same ones that occupied center stage in 1950. These are action studies in which "tradition" figures as one feature of the scene, but it is not always dominant and not always determinative. Perhaps most important of all, this is not an agentless anthropology of forces, cultural, economic, or whatever. These works constitute reports about specific persons, specific occurrences, and the intentions and justifications expressed during the events in which people participate.

Past and Future:
Conclusion and Recapitulation

THIS BOOK has provided a short review of a full history. The sheer quantity of ethnographic work has made the possibility of commentary an exercise not only in selection but also in self-restraint. The subspecializations of anthropology have proliferated to the point where they often have more in common with parallel topics in other disciplines than with other sectors within anthropology. Africa is itself so large, so complex, and so diverse that although some general, continentwide commonalities exist, there are many striking local differences. It follows that recent studies done by anthropologists in Africa can differ so much from one another in region, in topic, and in theoretical aim that they are only methodologically recognizable as contributing to a single pool of connected information. Their authors have three things in common— a knowledge of the earlier anthropological literature on Africa, a familiarity with the general theoretical problems addressed in the discipline, and a commitment to the fieldwork method. Most are also aware of the succession of critiques that have swirled around the academic enterprise. The on-the-ground work obviously continues apace along its separate specialized paths unobstructed by (or sometimes perhaps stimulated by) the critical commentary.

Did any form of criticism of anthropology exist in the "classic" period of Africanist fieldwork in the 1930 to 1960 period, when anthropologists seemed so confident? The answer is yes. At that time, Euro-American anthropologists had to contend with professional engagement in a topic that many considered marginal, perhaps not even worth pursuing. In the academy, the central story was that of the development of Euro-American high culture and the valorization of its products. Although other parts of the world were interesting curiosities, their cultures (and the people who studied them) lacked the same academic standing as those at the Euro-Anglo center. The current implications of this bias are well known, because they have produced a militant counterpolitics. The wide readership of Edward Said's 1979 commentary on "orientalism" and the upheavals over the curricula in the schools of the United States are common knowledge. Generally forgotten in the heat of such immediate concerns is that the anthropologists of the 1930–60 period should be credited with their contributions to legitimizing the serious academic study of the non-Euro-American world at a time when that was a much more difficult endeavor than it is now. To be sure, these scholars succeeded only in some quarters, but that they pulled it off at all is remarkable. They made a place for their subject and themselves in a number of universities, founded organizations and publications, reached a significant public, and developed an ongoing, recognized profession. It was no small achievement, despite the many reservations one may have now about the way they went about their work and the way they interpreted their research.

As these anthropologists saw it, they went to Africa to understand African ways of doing things, African lives, African societies, African ideas. They listened carefully to their African interlocutors. They were not there to tell the Africans what to do or what to think. Their agenda was not the same as that of the missionaries, the settlers, and the administrators. For the most part— although in some instances they certainly engaged in other kinds of activities— anthropologists generally took the posture that they were there to learn.

There is no doubt that their time and the ideas with which they came to their fieldwork shaped their interpretations, but the same remains true today. Transcending the conceptions of reality prevalent at a particular historical moment is not a simple act of will. It involves a concatenation of circumstances that free the thought of a particular individual or group. Creating the conditions to make that possible is not easy, and there is serious question whether anyone really knows just how to do it.

The early generations of Africanists saw the colonial presence as something about which they could do little, much as anthropologists today cannot change the regimes in the countries in which they work. When possible, anthropologists tried to put the African case forward as they saw it. Given their struggle to legitimate their intellectual interest in things African, it is ironic that their work should now become such a favorite object of attack.

Some African critics today reject the intermediary, the foreign anthropologist, and would prefer to be heard themselves. But there are those, well acquainted with the problem of ethnographic distortion, who argue that anthropology nonetheless has its uses. Thus, Christopher Miller says

> If anthropology has anything to offer the reader of African literatures, it is not just ethnographic "facts" but also access to modes of understanding that emanate from other cultures. . . . The grandest promise of anthropology is of gaining access to such systems through the supposedly transparent mediation of ethnographic texts. The inescapable epistemological paradox here is of course that access to non-Western systems is mediated through a discipline that has been invented and controlled by the West. My contention is that without a surrender to that paradox, without some reliance on anthropological texts, Westerners will not be able to read African literatures in any adequate way. (1990, 21)

Of course, ethnographic texts are not transparent. Of course, the intermediary knowingly or unconsciously will likely interpose interpretive glosses that African speakers might not put forward. But that does not by definition make the interpretation or the other parts of the ethnographic product worthless. A great deal has recently been written about alterity, about the Other, about seeing the world of non-Euro-Americans largely in terms of their differences from ourselves. That style of discourse was long imagined to be a fairly simple and candid way of talking about the familiar and the unfamiliar, the known and the unknown. It was seen as the result of using oneself as the principal instrument of research, a comment on the experience of fieldwork, not as the defining feature of the research problem.

Mention of difference is now sometimes treated critically as a deliberate distancing from the Other, tantamount to a refusal to recognize a common humanity. That seems a mischievous, calculated, political exaggeration. One could cite to the contrary the fact that critics of our own society periodically have chosen to justify anthropological studies of others because such projects will unsettle our naturalization of our own world (Benedict 1934; Lévi-Strauss 1974; Marcus and Fischer 1986). Although unobjectionable in its well-meaning intentions and commendable in its reversal of stereotypes about who is likely to learn from whom, that argument often remains remarkably self-centered and self-serving. Like other forms of knowledge, awareness of the particulars of the great range of human cultures and societies surely has many possible uses. Freeing ourselves from the idea that our cultural constructs are natural is an important one, but it is only one.

A less prescriptive conception of the goal may be more suitable to the long-term life of an inquiring discipline. A broader, more general vision of the anthropological project has existed for quite a while. In that view, ethnography does not principally constitute a source for a specific form of moral-philosophical enlightenment, a convenient platform on which to mount a critique of the West, or a way of perpetuating calumnies about the non-West. Instead, ethnography becomes an instrument for constructing a global archive of social observations, a knowledge bank of the great range of human social inventions in their enormous variety, a vast collection to expand the fragmentary story we now have and to try to understand it.

Why then, in the context of African studies, are there so often intimations in the American arena that social anthropology represents the worst genre of orientalist thinking? Are these accusations an outdated residue from arguments based on anthropology's origins in the colonial period from which so many people have made a postcolonial academic living? Or are they lodged in the history of academic learning in the West, which has so long overemphasized a self-congratulatory, conventionalized internal narrative of Western history against a possible history of the world? Or are they merely an expression of the current vagaries of sectoral politics in America? Africanist anthropologists, whatever their other faults, surely have been steadfast voices for more serious attention to the non-Western world and have provided scholarly examples of what they advocate.

But the noise made by these repetitive, stereotypical criticisms should not drown out the sound of more serious internal critiques, and defensiveness should not encourage a dug-in complacency. Ethnography today must take (and in many quarters is taking) a processual direction. Whatever other frameworks are used as well, ethnography must be fundamentally committed to a temporally conscious approach. This strategy involves deep awareness of the implications of the fact that academic models are temporary and the scenes that ethnographers observe are temporary. Africanist anthropology is not a special case in that regard, whether done by Africans or by outsiders. Awareness that a great deal of present ethnographic work is conceived as a kind of current history and thus is processual in orientation would not silence critics who claim that anthropology is static, but it might deprive the most florid exaggerators of a slice of their audience.

It is clear to everyone in the discipline that the "today" in which ethnographers involve themselves firsthand will be yesterday soon enough. Ethnographic observation and the accompanying dialogue explores events in a segment of time. If one talks with West Africans today knowing that in twenty-five years their population will most probably have doubled and that it has already doubled from what it was twenty-five years ago, one cannot see the moment of present contact "out of time." Dramatic demographic transformations are not the issue (although they serve nicely as an example of radical change). The anthropological attitude is and must be deeply conscious of the ethnographic moment as a passage between yesterday and tomorrow.

This stance has many methodological as well as theoretical implications. Concentrating on what is happening at the time of observation yet speculating on what there is about it that is dynamic, formative of the present, and possibly of the future involves a shift of emphasis from past anthropological preoccupations with customary practice and conventionalized cultural ideas and forms. The focus on the action, on what is moving, and on the ideas that surround it, on what is uncertain about the consequences, requires a pleasure in thought experiments. The core of this attitude is a fascination with possibility. Unfortunately for the training-manual-minded, there is no simple cookbook for such an objective, nor can there be. Considering events in a zone of possibilities requires curiosity, playfulness, luck, and tremendous patience. It also involves an initial willingness to dignify with possible significance virtually everything heard or observed. Interpreting it, sorting the signs, messages, and stories into important and unimportant in relation to a selected theme, is both a simultaneous and a subsequent activity, some of it conscious, some not, some of it done by the people in the arena of action, some of it by their observers and interlocutors.

Historians have the advantage of sequential data over a period of time. They know how the story came out. But anthropologists do not know for certain how it will end, and, moreover, they do not know from what source change (or sameness and replication) will come. Will it be generated locally, nationally, or regionally? Will it result from environmental or demographic change? From human agency? If so, who will be the significant actors?

The question formerly of central interest to anthropologists (and still so for some) was whether cultural forms and practices had logical systemic connections and whether they were reproduced from one generation to another. Only those practices that were reproduced, the durable "traditional" ones, held interest. The rest were transitory and consequently not culturally important. The scholars constructed the definition of the traditional out of two elements: what people told the anthropologist were age-old customs and what the anthropologist found exotic. The exotic was assumed to be traditional, because what was new was, by definition, presumed to emanate from the Western "modern" world and to be recognizable as such. Everything else was surely "traditional."

Anthropology is older and wiser now. It is clear that in all societies there are newly "invented" elements that are given legitimacy and prestige by being labeled traditional (see Hobsbawm and Ranger 1983). Local assertions of what is traditional are just that— assertions. They do not necessarily constitute an account of actual happenings in a historical past. There also are recently invented forms of exotica that look ancient to a foreigner but are not, in fact, at all old. But more than that, there are cultural artifacts and practices received from the non-African world that come to mean something entirely different in the African context in which they are used from what they mean in Winnetka.

Even when particular cultural ideas and forms of activity have been reproduced, handed down from one generation to the next, anthropologists need to know to what extent the context in which they are "replicated" has changed. Are the reproduced bits now part of a different aggregate, a new total complex, in which adherence to certain "traditional" practices has new political significance? What does it mean to retain "traditional" religion if everyone around you has converted to Islam? The meaning surely differs from the past. A salient example that has global referents is the use to which signals of ethnicity are put today. In Africa, as elsewhere, this is no simple nostalgia for the past; it is also mobilized in the service of present political alignments and is deftly folded in with attempts to configure the future.

Accompanying the emergent and increasing emphasis on process, there exists in anthropology today a noticeable fading of the earlier ambition to describe the totality of a "culture." For the most part, because of the change of perspective, cultural

contexts now seem too complex, too multileveled, too susceptible to shifts, and too full of variations of practice to capture as
totalities. Although the culture concept is seldom directly attacked, three topical themes show clearly how its old meanings
are currently subverted and changed. One of them is ethnicity,
the second is the idea of social field, and the third is identity.

The political importance of ethnicity, ethnic nationalism,
and nationalism is not a case that needs demonstration these
days, but what about its theoretical place? In anthropology, just
when many settings seemed to metamorphosize into culturally
mixed scenes that looked as if they never could or would separate into distinguishable cultural unities, the politics of ethnicity emerged in other places, setting boundaries and separat-
ing populations more rigidly than ever. For anthropological
theory, is "ethnicity" the avatar of "tribe"? Can the techniques and concepts that anthropology invented when it studied tribes translate at all to the new realities of ethnic politics in
plural arenas? The active agents and agencies of ethnic mobili-
zation are too much in evidence today for the idea of a cultural
tradition entrapping generation after generation through some
impersonal force of its own to dominate analysis.

The idea of "social field" also places the culture question (to
the extent that it arises at all) directly within a peopled milieu.
Because social fields have varying dimensions and their hold
over those who participate in them varies ethnographers are
obliged to fill in singularly open concepts as befits the special
circumstances of each field site. Thus, a tool of analysis makes
demands on ethnographers. To use it, they must inspect both
the reasons why particular people are involved in particular
social fields and the idiom in which that involvement is expressed. The "culture" special to a social field may well be an
object of interest, but the very idea of multiple social fields and
the possibility of multiple subcultural domains, of part cultures, substantially subverts the older totalizing and unitary
conception of culture.

As for "identity," now much used in anthropology, how do
its ambiguities assist in the construction of such modifications?

"Identity" encapsulates several quite different perspectives on persons and who they are. Two of these viewpoints stand out. In one sense, identity refers to being identical to others. In that sense, identity is a social concept about categories or groups of people who think of themselves (or are thought of by others) as alike in some significant way— i.e., in terms of tribal, ethnic, occupational, class, gender, subgroup, or other markers. In another sense, "identity" is about uniqueness, about individuality. The individual may be a composite of a variety of identity elements taken from diverse settings (or categories). Both of these meanings— identity as sameness and identity as individuality, identity as social membership and identity as individual configuration— serve the anthropologist. They represent techniques for integrating particular cultural constructions (or clusters of such constructions) into the characterizations of persons and their milieux without resorting to the description of a total "culture." This constitutes a strategy for placing ethnographic emphasis on the lodging of identities in persons rather than taking as the ethnographic goal the abstracting of norms or cultural systems as analytically separable entities, separated from their human bearers.

For an anthropologist working in Africa today, understanding events involves all of these issues and more. It involves both attempting to understand what is happening locally, before one's eyes, and simultaneously trying to place that knowledge in larger-scale terms. Or, to put scale in a temporal rather than a spatial frame, it also involves attempts to understand the visible in terms of pasts and futures, local and supralocal. Putting it all together is a big order, and the task highlights the importance of a type of ethnographic data that, although much used in practice, has not received the theoretical centrality it deserves: the unfolding of events. Events represent the fieldwork key to processual approaches, the action aspect of identities. The preferred events for study are, of course, those affected as little as possible by the anthropologist's presence. Whether the local impact of a change in the price of a cash crop, the playing out of a local dispute, or the performance of a ritual, the investigation of such specific and concrete matters gives an anchor in verifiable facts to explorations of the (probably diverse) meanings and interpretations ascribed to these events by the participants.

I have written about these methodological and theoretical matters elsewhere and this is not the place to expand further on this large topic. But to the extent that not only my own work but that of many other Africanist anthropologists has become processual and methodologically event-oriented (or incident-oriented), historically minded (even when the scholars are not writing histories), I think that some of the orientalist critiques of the discipline clearly are as out of date as the ideas attacked. But other skeptical and contestational evaluations are on the mark.

To recapitulate briefly: the history of professional anthropological involvement in Africa is the twentieth-century story that has been sketched here. Two overlapping themes animated much of that work: identifying, understanding, and comparing what were conceived of as local "traditions"; and addressing the changing current African experience. In the first half of the century, the two themes tended to be addressed separately. Synchronic ethnographic descriptions of specific traditional systems were objects of high intellectual interest. The less "Westernized" a people were, the more interesting they were. In 1969, soon after I started my work on Kilimanjaro, I spoke with one of the most senior British Africanists of the time. He said that he could not understand why I would want to study Chagga affairs. In one succinct remark he showed both his professional taste for the exotic and his ethnographic gender biases: "They are too modern," he said, "they probably all wear pants." Ethnography concerned a culturally uncontaminated Africa, and it concerned men.

I had, in fact, chosen to work among the Chagga precisely because, of all the rural peoples in Tanzania, they were among those most involved in the cash economy and in other non-traditional institutions. The learned professor said indirectly that in his view of the profession the "traditional" was the only material out of which comparative theories could be built. For him, "transforming" and "Europeanized" settings fitted into a different category altogether. Because of their mixed cultural provenance, they were not as much of academic interest as of practical use. A transforming Africa was for him a matter of "applied anthropology" usually associated with government policy. The professor considered neither policy nor change central to the discipline's intellectual problematic. In expressing these views, he did not represent everyone or even everyone of his generation. Perhaps he did not even represent himself in other, more serious moods.

The history reviewed in this work shows that many anthropologists considered the subject much more inclusive than he did well before 1960, let alone after that time. It was obvious to some quite early on that the ethnographic reconstruction of untouched "traditional" systems was something of an artificial exercise and that anthropology should also take account of actual complex contemporary scenes. A changing world had forced anthropology to reconsider its self-definition. African affairs played a significant role in this development.

For ethnographers today, what happens in Africa is African, whatever its cultural origin. The old overvaluation of the authentically indigenous and exotic has largely passed. The indigenous forms supposedly immune to external influence and free of changing circumstance are now left for the elegant coffee-table books of others. Anthropologists ply a different trade. The ongoing interaction between discipline and subject-matter is patent.

The new Africa that is just now emerging, the post–cold war Africa that is, as always, a mix of the heroic, the tragic, and the mundane, presents anthropology with new challenges— applied, practical, and theoretical. Anthropology may be poised for yet another phase of theoretical and methodological revision. What will be the involvement of African scholars in this effort? One hopes that it will be larger than it has been. During the colonial period and soon thereafter, a handful of Africans became anthropologists. Some published classical ethnographic monographs on their own peoples, others on other concerns, such as migration (see for example, Kenyatta 1938; Busia 1951; Danquah 1928, 1968; Deng 1971, 1972; Diop 1965, 1979). These men were trained in a British or European tradition and wrote very much in the intellectual style of the countries from which they received their degrees. Will the new generation of African anthropologists be differently formed?

The postindependence era did not at first bring an increased surge of interest in anthropology on the part of Africans. Quite the contrary, in many places anthropology fell into political disfavor. Many African universities banished the subject. The discipline was regarded with suspicion both because of its association with the colonial period and because, given its snooping and inquiring habits, embarrassing and inconvenient things might come to light. Not surprisingly, the group of Africans trained as anthropologists remained small, but it is now growing. The numbers are now sufficient so that a Pan-African Association of Anthropologists has recently been launched (see References Cited). A new generation of African anthropologists and sociologists is ready to make its mark in what is now a much broader international arena than before. Today scholars from many countries in addition to France, Britain, and the United States (including Sweden, Finland, Germany, the Netherlands, and Japan) have a strong interest in Africanist research (see, for example, Peek 1990, on Japan; Schott 1982, on German legal anthropology; Binsbergen 1982, on Dutch anthropology). The fact that an ever more inclusive international community is engaged in African studies should serve as a useful defense against parochial interpretations. Meanwhile, a fin-de-siècle ethnography of Africa will begin its twenty-first-century work as a form of current history— until it becomes something else.

References Cited

Adler, Alfred, et al. 1986. *Afrique plurielle, Afrique actuelle: Hommage à Georges Balandier.* Paris: Karthala.

Allott, A. N. 1969. "The Restatement of African Law Project of the School of Oriental and African Studies, London: A General Report on the Period 1959–1969." Mimeo.

Ankermann, B. 1905. "Kulturkreise und Kulturschichten in Ozeanien and Afrika." *Zeitschrift fur Ethnologie* 37:54–84.

Augé, Marc. 1969. *Le rivage Alladian.* Paris: Orstom.

——. 1975. *Théorie des pouvoirs et idéologie.* Paris: Hermann.

——. 1977. *Pouvoirs de vie, pouvoirs de mort.* Paris: Flammarion.

——. 1979. *Symbole, fonction, histoire.* Paris: Hachette.

——. 1982. *The Anthropological Circle: Symbol, Function, History.* Cambridge: Cambridge University Press.

Augé, Marc, and Claudine Herzlich. 1984. *Le sens du mal: Anthropologie, histoire, sociologie de la maladie.* Montreux: Éditions des Archives Contemporaires.

Balandier, Georges. 1955. *Sociologie des Brazzavilles noires.* Paris: A. Colin.

——. 1957. *Afrique ambiguë.* Paris: Plon.

——. 1960. "The French Tradition of African Research." *Human Organization* 19:108–11.

——, ed. [1955] 1963. *Sociologie actuelle de l'Afrique noire.* Paris: Presses universitaires de France.

——. 1970. *Political Anthropology.* New York: Vintage Books, Random House.

——. 1974. *Anthropo-logiques.* Paris: Presses universitaires de France.

——. 1977. *Histoire d'autres.* Paris: Stock.

Banton, Michael. 1957. *West African City.* London: Oxford University Press.

——. 1965. "Social Alignment and Identity in a West African City." In *Urbanization and Migration in West Africa,* Hilda Kuper, ed., 163–85. Berkeley and Los Angeles: University of California Press.

Barley, Nigel. 1983. *Symbolic Structures: An Exploration of the Culture of the Dowayos.* Cambridge: Cambridge University Press.

References Cited

Barnes, S. 1986. *Patrons and Power: Creating a Political Community in Metropolitan Lagos*. Bloomington: Indiana University Press.

Bascom, W. R., and M. Herskovits. 1959. *Continuity and Change in African Cultures*. Chicago: University of Chicago Press.

Bascom, William. 1962. "Some Aspects of Yoruba Urbanization." *American Anthropologist* 64:699–709.

———. "The Urban African and His World." 1963. *Cahiers d'Études Africaines* 14:163–85.

Bates, Robert. 1981. *Markets and States in Tropical Africa*. Berkeley and Los Angeles: University of California Press.

———, ed. 1993. *Anthropology and the Disciplines*. Chicago: University of Chicago Press.

Bauman, H., et al. 1943. *Volkerkunde von Afrika*. Essen: Essener Verlagsanhalt.

Baxter, P., and Uri Almagor, eds. 1978. *Age, Generation, and Time: Some Features of East African Age Organization*. New York: St. Martin's Press.

Bay, Edna G. 1982. *Women and Work in Africa*. Boulder, Colo.: Westview Press.

Beattie, J. H. M. 1971. *The Nyoro State*. London: Oxford University Press.

Beattie, J. H. M., and J. Middleton, eds. 1969. *Spirit Mediumship and Society in Africa*. New York: Africana.

Beidelman, T. O. 1968. "Some Nuer Notions of Nakedness, Nudity, and Sexuality." *Africa* 38:113–32.

———. 1974. "Social Theory and the Study of Christian Missions." *Africa* 44:235–49.

———. 1982. *Colonial Evangelism*. Bloomington: Indiana University Press.

———. 1986. *Moral Imagination in Kaguru Modes of Thought*. Bloomington: Indiana University Press.

Benedict, Ruth. 1934. *Patterns of Culture*. Boston: Houghton Mifflin.

Besmer, F., 1983. *Horses, Musicians, and Gods: The Hausa Cult of Possession Trance*. South Hadley, Mass.: Bergin and Garvey.

Binsbergen, Wim M. J. van. 1981. *Religious Change in Zambia*. London and Boston: Kegan Paul International.

———. 1982. *Dutch Anthropology of Sub-Saharan Africa in the 1970s*. Leiden, the Netherlands: African Studies Centre.

———. 1992. *Tears of Rain: Ethnicity and History in Central Western Zambia*. London and New York: Kegan Paul International.

Binsbergen, Wim M. J. van, and Matthew Schoffeleers, eds. 1985. *Theoretical Explorations in African Religion*. London and Boston: Kegan Paul International.

Bledsoe, C. M. 1980. *Women and Marriage in Kpelle Society.* Stanford, Calif.: Stanford University Press.

Bloch, Maurice. 1977. "The Past and the Present in the Present." *Man* 12:278–92.

——, ed. 1984. *Marxist Analyses and Social Anthropology.* London and New York: Tavistock.

Bohannan, Paul. 1953. *The Tiv of Central Nigeria.* London: International African Institute.

——. 1954. *Tiv Farm and Settlement.* Colonial Research Studies, no. 15. London: H. M. Stationery Office.

——. 1955. "Some Principles of Exchange and Investment among the Tiv." *American Anthropologist* 57:60–70.

——. 1957. *Justice and Judgment among the Tiv.* London: Oxford University Press.

——. 1959. "The Impact of Money on an African Subsistence Economy." *Journal of Economic History* 19:491–503.

Bohannan, Paul, and Laura Bohannan. 1968. *Tiv Economy.* Evanston, Ill.: Northwestern University Press.

Bohannan, Paul, and George Dalton. 1962. *Markets in Africa.* Evanston, Ill.: Northwestern University Press.

Bond, G. C. 1976. *The Politics of Change in a Zambian Community.* Chicago: University of Chicago Press.

Bourdieu, Pierre. 1977. *Outline of a Theory of Practice.* New York: Cambridge University Press.

Bourdillon, M. F. 1971. "Some Aspects of the Religion of the Eastern Korekore." D. Phil. thesis, Oxford University.

——. 1979. "The Cults of Dzivaguru and Karuva amongst the North-East Shona peoples." In *Guardians of the Land: Essays on Central African Territorial Cults,* ed. J. M. Schoffeleers, 235–55. Gwelo, Zimbabwe: Mambo Press.

——. 1981. "Suggestions of Bureaucracy in Korekore Religion: Putting 'the Ethnography Straight.'" *Zambezia* 10:119–36.

——. 1982. "Freedom and Constraint among Shona Spirit Mediums." In *Religious Organization and Religious Experience,* ed., J. Davis, 181–94. ASA Monograph. London: Academic Press.

Brown, Richard. 1973. "Anthropology and Colonial Rule: The Case of Godfrey Wilson and the Rhodes-Livingstone Institute, Northern Rhodesia." In *Anthropology and the Colonial Encounter,* ed. Talal Asad, 173–97. London: Ithaca Press.

Buckley, Anthony D. 1985. *Yoruba Medicine.* Oxford: Clarendon Press.

Burnham, Philip. 1980. *Opportunity and Constraint in a Savanna Society: The Gbaya of Cameroon.* London: Academic Press.

References Cited

Busia, K. A. 1951. *The Position of the Chief in the Modern Political System of the Ashanti.* London: Oxford University Press for the International African Institute.

Buxton, J. 1963. *Chiefs and Strangers.* Oxford: Clarendon Press.

———. 1972. *Religion and Healing in Mandari.* London: Oxford University Press.

Chanock, Martin. 1985. *Law, Custom, and Social Order.* Cambridge: Cambridge University Press.

Chayanov, A. V. 1966. *The Theory of Peasant Economy.* Homewood, Ill.: Richard D. Irwin for the American Economic Association.

Clifford, James. 1988. *The Predicament of Culture.* Cambridge: Harvard University Press.

Clifford, James, and George E. Marcus, eds. 1986. *Writing Culture: The Poetics and Politics of Ethnography.* Berkeley and Los Angeles: University of California Press.

Cock, J. 1980. *Maids and Madams: A Study in the Politics of Exploitation.* Johannesburg: Ravan Press.

Cohen, Abner. 1969. *Custom and Politics in Urban Africa.* London: Routledge and Kegan Paul.

———. 1981. *The Politics of Elite Culture: Explorations in the Dramaturgy of Power in a Modern African Society.* Berkeley and Los Angeles: University of California Press.

Cohen, David William. 1972. *The Historical Tradition of Busoga.* Oxford: Clarendon.

———. 1977. *Wominafu's Binafu: A Study of Authority in a Nineteenth-Century African Community.* Princeton: Princeton University Press.

———. 1989. *Siaya: The Historical Anthropology of an African Landscape.* London: J. Currey; Athens: Ohio University Press.

———. 1992. *Burying SM: The Politics of Knowledge and the Sociology of Power in Africa.* Portsmouth, N.H.: Heineman; London: Currey.

Cohen, Ronald, and John Middleton, eds. 1970. *From Tribe to Nation in Africa.* Scranton, Pa.: Chandler Publishing Co.

Colson, Elizabeth. 1948. "Rain Shrines of the Plateau Tonga of Northern Rhodesia." *Africa* 18:272–83.

———. 1953. "Social Control and Vengeance in Plateau Tonga Society." *Africa* 23:199–212.

———. 1958. *Marriage and Family among the Plateau Tonga of Northern Rhodesia.* Manchester: Manchester University Press.

———. 1960a. "Migration in Africa: Trends and Possibilities." In *Population in Africa,* ed. F. Lorimer and M. Karp, 60–67. Boston: Boston University Press.

——. 1960b. *Social Organisation of the Gwembe Tonga*. Manchester: Manchester University Press.

——. 1962. *The Plateau Tonga of Northern Rhodesia: Social and Religious Studies*. Manchester: Manchester University Press.

——. 1971. *The Social Consequences of Resettlement*. Manchester: Manchester University Press for the Institute of African Studies, University of Zambia.

——. 1976. "From Chief's Court to Local Court: The Evolution of Local Courts in Zambia." *Political Anthropology* 1:15–29.

Colson, Elizabeth, and Max Gluckman, eds. 1951. *Seven Tribes of British Central Africa*. Oxford: Oxford University Press for the Rhodes-Livingstone Institute.

Colson, Elizabeth, and Thayer Scudder. 1975. "New Economic Relationships between the Gwembe Valley and the Line of Rail." In *Town and Country in East and Central Africa*, ed. David Parkin, 190–210. London: International African Institute.

——. 1988. *For Prayer and Profit: The Ritual, Economic, and Social Importance of Beer in Gwembe District, Zambia, 1950–1982*. Stanford, Calif.: Stanford University Press.

Comaroff, Jean. 1985. *Body of Power, Spirit of Resistance*. Chicago: University of Chicago Press.

Comaroff, Jean, and John Comaroff. 1991. *Of Revelation and Revolution: Christianity, Colonialism, and Consciousness in South Africa*. Chicago: University of Chicago Press.

Comaroff, John L., ed. 1980. *The Meaning of Marriage Payments*. New York: Academic Press.

Comaroff, John L., and Simon Roberts. 1981. *Rules and Processes: The Cultural Logic of Dispute in an African Context*. Chicago: University of Chicago Press.

Cooper, Frederick. 1981. "Africa and the World Economy." *African Studies Review* 24:1–86.

Copans, Jean. 1977. "African Studies: A Periodization." In *African Social Studies*. Peter C. W. Gutkind ed. and Peter Waterman, 11–31. New York and London: Monthly Review Press.

——. 1980. *Les marabouts de l'arachide*. Paris: Sycomore.

Coquery-Vidrovitch, C. 1969. "Recherches sur une mode de production Africain." *La Pensée* 144:61–78.

——. 1983. *Enterprises et entrepreneurs en Afrique*. Paris: Harmattan.

——. 1988. *Processus d'urbanisation en Afrique*. 2 vols. Paris: Harmattan.

——. 1991. "The Process of Urbanization in Africa." *African Studies Review* 34:1–98.

Cruise O'Brien, D. 1975. *Saints and Politicians: Essays in the Organization of a Senegalese Peasant Society.* Cambridge: Cambridge University Press.

Daneel, M. L. 1971, 1974. *Old and New in Shona Independent Churches.* 2 vols. The Hague: Mouton for Afrika-Studiecentrum.

Danquah, J. B. 1928. *Akan Laws and Customs and the Akim Abuakwa Constitution.* London: Routledge.

——. 1968. *The Akan Doctrine of God.* London: Cass.

Deble, I., and P. Hugon. 1982. *Vivre et survivre dans les villes Africaines.* Paris: Presses universitaires de France.

DeHeusch, Luc. 1958. *Essais sur le symbolisme de l'inceste royal en Afrique.* Brussels: Institut de Sociologie Solvay.

——. 1972. *Le roi ivre.* Paris: Gallimard.

——. 1985. *Sacrifice in Africa.* Manchester: Manchester University Press.

Deng, F. M. 1971. *Tradition and Modernization: A Challenge for Law among the Dinka of the Sudan.* New Haven: Yale University Press.

——. 1972. *The Dinka of the Sudan.* New York: Holt, Rinehart, and Winston.

Dike, K. Onwuka. 1963. "In Memoriam: Melville Jean Herskovits." *African Studies Bulletin* 6:1–3.

Diop, Abdoulaye Bara. 1965. *Société toucouleur et migration.* Initiations et études Africaines (séries sans périodicité fixe), no. 18. Dakar: Institut Français d'Afrique noir.

——. 1979. *La société Wolof: Tradition et changement.* 2 vols. Université de Paris. Mimeo.

——. 1981. *La société Wolof: Les systèmes d'inégalité et de domination.* Paris: Karthala.

——. 1985. *La famille Wolof: Tradition et changement.* Paris: Karthala.

Donham, Donald. 1985. *Work and Power in Maale, Ethiopia.* Ann Arbor, Mich.: UMI Research Press.

——. 1990. *History, Power, Ideology.* Cambridge: Cambridge University Press.

Douglas, Mary. 1963. *The Lele of the Kasai.* London, Ibadan, and Accra: Oxford University Press for the International African Institute.

——. 1966. *Purity and Danger.* New York: Praeger.

——. 1970. *Natural Symbols: Explorations in Cosmology.* New York: Pantheon Books.

——, ed. 1973. *Rules and Meanings.* Harmondsworth, England: Penguin Education.

——. 1981. *Edward Evans-Pritchard*. Harmondsworth, England: Penguin Books.

Downs, R. E., and S. P. Reyna, eds. 1988. *Land and Society in Contemporary Africa*. Hanover and London: University Press of New England.

Dupré, Georges, and P. P. Rey. 1969. "Reflexions sur la pertinence d'une théorie des échanges." *Cahiers Internationaux de Sociologie* 46:133–62.

Durkheim, Emile. [1912] 1961. *The Elementary Forms of Religious Life*. New York: Collier Books.

——. [1895] 1962. *The Rules of Sociological Method*. New York: Free Press of Glencoe.

——. [1893] 1966. *The Division of Labor in Society*. New York: Free Press of Glencoe.

Dyson-Hudson, N. 1966. *Karimojong Politics*. Oxford: Clarendon Press.

Eades, J., ed. 1987. *Migrants, Workers, and the Social Order*. London: Tavistock.

Economist, September 25, 1993: 49–50, Survey 6–44.

Epstein, A. L. 1958. *Politics in an Urban African Community*. Manchester: Manchester University Press.

——, ed. 1967a. *The Craft of Social Anthropology*. London: Tavistock.

——. 1967b. "Urbanization and Social Change in Africa." *Current Anthropology* 8:275–95.

Ethnographic Survey of Africa. 1945–. London: International African Institute.

Etienne, Mona, and E. Leacock, eds. 1980. *Women and Colonization: Anthropological Perspectives*. New York: Praeger.

Evans-Pritchard, E. E. 1934. "Lévy-Bruhl's Theory of Primitive Mentality." *Bulletin, Faculty of Arts* (Cairo, Egypt: Farouk University) 2:1–36.

——. 1937. *Witchcraft, Oracles, and Magic among the Azande*. Oxford: Clarendon Press.

——. 1940a. *The Nuer*. Oxford: Clarendon Press.

——. 1940b. *The Political System of the Anuak of the Anglo-Egyptian Sudan*. London: Percy Lund Humphries and Co.

——. 1949. *The Sanusi of Cyrenaica*. Oxford: Clarendon Press.

——. 1951. *Kinship and Marriage among the Nuer*. Oxford: Clarendon Press.

——. 1956. *Nuer Religion*. Oxford: Clarendon Press.

——. 1962. *Social Anthropology and Other Essays*. New York: Free Press of Glencoe.

References Cited

Fabian, Johannes. 1983. *Time and the Other: How Anthropology Makes Its Object*. New York: Columbia University Press.

Fallers, Lloyd. 1956. *Bantu Bureaucracy*. Cambridge, England: Heffer for the East African Institute of Social Research.

———. 1964. *The King's Men*. London: Oxford University Press.

Fardon, Richard, ed. 1990. *Localizing Strategies*. Edinburgh and Washington: Scottish Academic Press and Smithsonian Institution Press.

Feierman, Steven. 1974. *The Shambaa Kingdom*. Madison: University of Wisconsin Press.

———. 1979. *Health and Society in Africa: A Working Bibliography*. Waltham, Mass.: Crossroads Press.

———. 1990. *Peasant Intellectuals*. Madison: University of Wisconsin Press.

Ferguson, James. 1990. *The Anti-Politics Machine*. Cambridge: Cambridge University Press.

Fernandez, J. W. 1974. "The Mission of Metaphor in Expressive Culture." *Current Anthropology* 15:119–45.

———. 1978. "African Religious Movements." *Annual Review of Anthropology* 7:195–234.

———. 1979. "Africanization, Europeanization, Christianization." *History of Religions* 18:284–92.

———. 1982. *Bwiti: An Ethnography of the Religious Imagination in Africa*. Princeton: Princeton University Press.

Feuchtwang, Stephan. 1973. "The Discipline and Its Sponsors." In *Anthropology and the Colonial Encounter*, ed. Talal Asad, 71–100. London: Ithaca Press.

Firth, Raymond. 1947. "Social Problems and Research in British West Africa." *Africa* 17:77–91, 170–79.

———. 1951. *Elements of Social Organization*. London: Watts.

Forde, C. Daryll. 1934. *Habitat, Economy, and Society*. London: Methuen.

———. 1937. "Social Change in a West African Village Community." *Man* 37:10–13.

———. 1939. "Government in Umor: A Study of Social Change and Problems of Indirect Rule in a Nigerian Village Community." *Africa* 12:129–62.

———. 1953. "Applied Anthropology in Government: British Africa." In *Anthropology Today*, ed. A. L. Kroeber, 841–65. Chicago: University of Chicago Press.

———, ed. 1954. *African Worlds*. London: Oxford University Press.

———. 1956a. *Efik Traders of Old Calabar*. London: Oxford University Press.

—— , ed. 1956b. *Social Implications of Industrialization and Urbanization in Africa South of the Sahara*. Paris: UNESCO.

—— . 1964. *Yako Studies*. London: Oxford University Press.

Forde, C. Daryll, and P. Kaberry, eds. 1967. *West African Kingdoms of the Nineteenth Century*. Cambridge: Cambridge University Press.

Forde, C. Daryll, and R. Scott. 1946. *The Native Economies of Nigeria*. London: H. M. Stationery Office.

Fortes, Meyer. 1936. "Culture Contact as a Dynamic Process." *Africa* 9:24–55.

—— . 1945. *The Dynamics of Clanship among the Tallensi*. London: Oxford University Press.

—— . 1949a. "Time and Social Structure: An Ashanti Case Study." In *Social Structure: Studies Presented to A. R. Radcliffe-Brown,* ed. Fortes, 1–32. Oxford: Clarendon.

—— . 1949b. *The Web of Kinship among the Tallensi*. London: Oxford University Press.

—— . 1953. "The Structure of Unilineal Descent Groups." *American Anthropologist* 55:17–41.

—— . 1970. *Kinship and the Social Order*. London: Routledge and Kegan Paul (1969 Chicago: Aldine).

—— . [1959] 1983. *Oedipus and Job in West African Religion*. Cambridge, London, and New York: Cambridge University Press.

—— . 1987. *Religion, Morality, and the Person: Essays on Tallensi Religion*. Edited and with an introduction by Jack Goody. Cambridge and New York: Cambridge University Press.

Fortes, Meyer, and Germaine Dieterlen, eds. 1965. *African Systems of Thought*. London: Oxford University Press.

Fortes, Meyer, and E. E. Evans-Pritchard, eds. 1940. *African Political Systems*. London: Oxford University Press.

Freund, Bill. 1988. *The African Worker*. Cambridge: Cambridge University Press.

Garbett, G. K. 1966. "Religious Aspects of Political Succession among the Valley Korekore." In *The Zambesian Past: Studies in Central African History,* ed. E. Stokes and R. Brown, 137–70. Manchester: Manchester University Press.

—— . 1969. "Spirit Mediums as Mediators in Valley Korekore Society." In *Spirit Mediumship in Africa,* ed. J. Beattie and J. Middleton, 104–27. New York: Africana.

—— . 1977. "Disparate Regional Cults and a Unitary Field in Zimbabwe." In *Regional Cults,* ed. R. Werbner, ASA Monographs, no. 16. London: Academic Press, 55–92.

Geschiere, Peter. 1982. *Village Communities and the State: Changing*

Relations among the Maka of South-Eastern Cameroon since the Colonial Conquest. Trans. James Ravell. London and Boston: Routledge and Kegan Paul.

Gluckman, Max. 1940. "Analysis of a Social Situation in Modern Zululand." *Bantu Studies* 14:1–30, 147–74. (Reprinted as Rhodes-Livingstone Institute Paper no. 28. Livingstone, Northern Rhodesia: Rhodes-Livingstone Institute, 1958.)

———. 1941. *Economy of the Central Barotse Plain.* Rhodes-Livingstone Papers, no. 7. Livingstone, Northern Rhodesia: Rhodes-Livingstone Institute.

———. 1942. "Some Processes of Social Change, Illustrated with Zululand Data." *African Studies* 1:243–60. (Reprinted as Rhodes-Livingstone Paper no. 28. Livingstone, Northern Rhodesia: Rhodes-Livingstone Institute, 1958.)

———. 1943a. *Administrative Organization of the Barotse Native Authorities.* Rhodes-Livingstone Institute Communications, no. 10. Livingstone, Northern Rhodesia: Rhodes-Livingstone Institute.

———. 1943b. *Essays on Lozi Land and Royal Property.* Rhodes-Livingstone Papers, no. 10. Livingstone, Northern Rhodesia: Rhodes-Livingstone Institute.

———. 1949. "The Village Headman in British Central Africa." *Africa* 19:89–101.

———. 1955. *The Judicial Process among the Barotse of Northern Rhodesia.* Manchester: Manchester University Press.

———. 1958. "Foreword." In *Tribal Cohesion in a Money Economy: A Study of the Mambwe People of Northern Rhodesia,* by William Watson, v–xvi. Manchester: Manchester University Press for the Rhodes-Livingstone Institute.

———. 1961. "Anthropological Problems Arising from the African Industrial Revolution." In *Social Change in Modern Africa,* ed. Aidan Southall, 67–82. London: Oxford University Press for the International African Institute.

———. 1965. *The Ideas in Barotse Jurisprudence.* New Haven: Yale University Press.

———. 1975. "Anthropology and Apartheid: The Work of South African Anthropologists." In *Studies in African Social Anthropology,* ed. M. Fortes and S. Patterson, 21–40. London: Academic Press.

Goody, E. 1982a. *From Craft to Industry: The Ethnography of Proto-Industrial Cloth Production.* Cambridge: Cambridge University Press.

———. 1982b. *Parenthood and Social Reproduction: Fostering and Oc-*

cupational Roles in West Africa. Cambridge: Cambridge University Press.

Goody, Jack, ed. 1958. *The Developmental Cycle in Domestic Groups*. Cambridge: Cambridge University Press.

——. 1961. "Religion and Ritual: The Definitional Problem." *British Journal of Sociology* 12:142–64.

——. 1962. *Death, Property, and the Ancestors: A Study of the Mortuary Customs of the Lodagaa of West Africa*. London: Tavistock.

——. 1967. *The Social Organization of the LoWiili*. 2d ed. London: Oxford University Press for the International African Institute.

——. 1968. *Literacy in Traditional Society*. Cambridge: Cambridge University Press.

——. 1969. *Comparative Studies in Kinship*. Stanford, Calif.: Stanford University Press.

——. 1971. *Technology, Tradition, and the State in Africa*. London: Oxford University Press.

——. 1972. *The Myth of the Bagre*. London: Oxford University Press.

——, ed. 1973. *The Character of Kinship*. Cambridge: Cambridge University Press.

——. 1976. *Production and Reproduction: A Comparative Study of the Domestic Domain*. Cambridge: Cambridge University Press.

——. 1977. *The Domestication of the Savage Mind*. Cambridge: Cambridge University Press.

——, ed. [1966] 1979. *Succession to High Office*. Cambridge: Cambridge University Press.

——. 1982. *Cooking, Cuisine, and Class*. Cambridge: Cambridge University Press.

——. 1986a. *The Interface between the Written and the Oral*. Cambridge: Cambridge University Press.

——. 1986b. *The Logic of Writing and the Organization of Society*. Cambridge: Cambridge University Press.

——. 1990a. *The Development of the Family and Marriage in Europe*. Cambridge: Cambridge University Press.

——. 1990b. *The Oriental, the Ancient, and the Primitive: Systems of Marriage and the Family in the Pre-Industrial Societies of Eurasia*. Cambridge: Cambridge University Press.

——. 1992. *The Culture of Flowers*. Cambridge: Cambridge University Press.

Goody, Jack, and S. J. Tambiah, eds. 1973. *Bridewealth and Dowry*. Cambridge: Cambridge University Press.

Green, M. 1941. *Land Tenure in an Ibo Village*. Monographs on Social Anthropology, no. 6. London: London School of Economics.

———. 1947. *Ibo Village Affairs*. London: Sidgwick and Jackson; New York: Praeger.

Griaule, Marcel. 1948. *Dieu d'eau: Entretiens avec Ogotemmêli*. Trans. 1965 as *Conversations with Ogotemmêli: An Introduction to Dogon Religious Ideas*. London: Oxford University Press for the International African Institute.

Griaule, Marcel, and Germaine Dieterlen. 1965. *Le renard pale*. Paris: Institut d'ethnologie.

Gugler, Josef. 1969. "On the Theory of Rural-Urban Migration: The Case of Subsaharan Africa." In *Migration,* ed. J. A. Jackson, 134–55. Sociological Studies, no. 2. Cambridge: Cambridge University Press.

———. 1971. "Life in a Dual System: Eastern Nigerians in Town, 1961." *Cahiers d'Etudes Africaines* 11:400–429.

Gugler, Josef, and William G. Flanagan, eds. 1978. *Urbanization and Social Change in West Africa*. Cambridge: Cambridge University Press.

Gulliver, Philip. 1955a. *The Family Herds: A Study of Two Pastoral Tribes in East Africa, the Jie and Turkana*. London: Routledge and Kegan Paul.

———. 1955b. *Labour Migration in a Rural Economy*. E. A. Studies, no. 6. Kampala, Uganda: East African Institute of Social Research.

———. 1958. *Land Tenure and Social Change among the Nyakyasa: A Study of the Ngoni and Ndendeuli of Southern Tanganyika*. E. A. Studies, no. 11. Kampala, Uganda: East African Institute of Social Research.

———. 1963. *Social Control in an African Society*. London: Routledge and Kegan Paul.

———. 1965. "Anthropology." In *The African World: A Survey of Social Research,* ed. Robert A. Lystad, 57–105. New York: Praeger.

———, ed., 1969. *Tradition and Transition in East Africa*. Berkeley and Los Angeles: University of California Press.

———. 1971. *Neighbors and Networks*. Berkeley and Los Angeles: University of California Press.

Gutkind, Peter C. W. 1974. *Urban Anthropology*. Assen, the Netherlands: Van Gorcum.

Gutkind, Peter C. W., and Immanuel Wallerstein, eds. 1985. *Political Economy of Contemporary Africa*. Beverly Hills: Sage.

Gutmann, Bruno. 1926. *Das Recht der Dschagga*. Munich.

Guyer, Jane. 1980. "Food, Cocoa, and the Division of Labor by Sex in Two West African Societies." *Comparative Studies in Society and History* 22:355–73.

———. 1981. "Household and Community in African Studies." *African Studies Review* 24:87–137.

———. 1984a. *Family and Farm in Southern Cameroon.* African Research Studies, no. 15. Boston: Boston University African Studies Center.

———. 1984b. "Naturalism in Models of African Production." *Man* 19:371–88.

———. 1986. "Indigenous Currencies and the History of Marriage Payments: A Case from Cameroon." *Cahiers d'Etudes Africaines* 104:577–610.

———, ed. 1987. *Feeding African Cities.* Manchester: Manchester University Press for the International African Institute.

———. 1988. "The Multiplication of Labor: Historical Methods in the Study of Gender and Agricultural Change in Modern Africa." *Current Anthropology* 29:247–72.

———. 1991. "Female Farming in Anthropology and African History." In *Gender at the Crossroads of Knowledge: Feminist Anthropology in the Postmodern Era,* ed. Micaela di Leonardo, 257–77. Berkeley and Los Angeles: University of California Press.

Hannerz, Ulf. 1980. *Exploring the City: Inquiries towards an Urban Anthropology.* New York: Columbia University Press.

———. 1987. "The World in Creolization." *Africa* 57:546–59.

Hansen, K. 1989. *Distant Companions: Servants and Employers in Zambia 1900–1985.* Ithaca: Cornell University Press.

Harms, Robert W. 1981. *River of Wealth, River of Sorrow: The Central Zaire Basin in the Era of the Slave and Ivory Trade, 1500–1891.* New Haven: Yale University Press.

———. 1987. *Games against Nature: An Eco-Cultural History of the Nunu of Equatorial Africa.* Cambridge and New York: Cambridge University Press.

Harris, Grace G. 1978. *Casting Out Anger.* Cambridge: Cambridge University Press.

Harris, Marvin. 1968. *The Rise of Anthropological Theory.* New York: Thomas Y. Crowell Co.

Hart, Keith. 1971. "Migration and Tribal Identity among the Frafras of Ghana." *Journal of Asian and African Studies* 6:21–36.

———. 1973. "Informal Income Opportunities and Urban Employment in Ghana." *Journal of Modern African Studies* 11:61–89.

———. 1982. *The Political Economy of West African Agriculture.* Cambridge: Cambridge University Press.

———. 1985. "Social Anthropology of West Africa." *Annual Review of Anthropology* 14:243–72.

References Cited

Heald, Suzette. 1989. *Controlling Anger: The Sociology of Gisu Violence*. Manchester and New York: Manchester University Press and Saint Martin's Press.

Hellmann, Ellen. 1935. "Methods of Urban Fieldwork." *Bantu Studies* 9:185–202.

——. 1937. "The Native in the Towns." *The Bantu Speaking Tribes of South Africa,* ed. I. Schapera, 405–34. London: Routledge.

——. 1948. *Rooiyard: A Sociological Study of an Urban Slum Yard.* Rhodes-Livingstone Paper no. 13. Cape Town: Oxford University Press.

——. 1949. "Urban Areas." In *Handbook on Race Relations in South Africa,* ed. Hellmann, 229–74. London: Oxford University Press.

Herskovits, Melville. 1926. "The Cattle-Complex in East Africa." *American Anthropologist* 28:230–72, 362–80, 949, 528, 633–64.

——. 1930. "The Culture Areas of Africa." *Africa* 3:59–77.

——. 1938. *Dahomey, an Ancient African Kingdom.* 2 vols. New York: J. J. Augustin.

Hill, Polly. 1963. *The Migrant Cocoa Farmers of Southern Ghana: A Study in Rural Capitalism.* Cambridge: Cambridge University Press.

——. 1977. *Population, Prosperity, and Poverty: Rural Kano, 1900–1970.* Cambridge: Cambridge University Press.

——. 1986. *Development Economics on Trial: The Anthropological Case for a Prosecution.* Cambridge: Cambridge University Press.

Hobsbawm, E., and T. Ranger, eds. 1983. *The Invention of Tradition.* Cambridge: Cambridge University Press.

Holleman, J. F. 1952. *Shona Customary Law.* Cape Town: Oxford University Press.

——. 1969. *Chief, Council, and Commissioner.* Assen, the Netherlands: Royal Van Gorcum Ltd. for Afrika-Studiecentrum.

Holy, Ladislav. 1991. *Religion and Custom in a Muslim Society: The Berti of Sudan.* Cambridge: Cambridge University Press.

Hopkins, A. G. 1973. *An Economic History of West Africa.* New York: Columbia University Press.

Hopkins, Nicholas S. 1972. *Popular Government in an African Town: Kita, Mali.* Chicago: University of Chicago Press.

Horowitz, Michael M., and Thomas Painter, eds. 1986. *Anthropology and Rural Development in West Africa.* London: Westview Press, Aldershot.

Horton, Robin. 1967. "African Traditional Thought and Western Science." *Africa* 37:50–71, 155–87.

——. 1971. "African Conversion." *Africa* 41:85–108.

———. 1975. "On the Rationality of Conversion." *Africa* 45:219–35, 373–99.

Hunter, Monica. 1936. *Reaction to Conquest*. London: Oxford University Press.

Iliffe, John. 1969. *Tanganyika under German Rule, 1905–1912*. London: Cambridge University Press.

———. 1979. *A Modern History of Tanganyika*. Cambridge and New York: Cambridge University Press.

———. 1987. *The African Poor*. Cambridge and New York: Cambridge University Press.

Jackson, Michael. 1977. *The Kuranko: Dimensions of Social Reality in a West African Society*. London: C. Hurst.

———. 1989. *Paths toward a Clearing*. Bloomington and Indianapolis: Indiana University Press.

James, Wendy. 1973. "The Anthropologist as Reluctant Imperialist." In *Anthropology and the Colonial Encounter*, ed. Talal Asad, 41–69. London: Ithaca Press.

———. 1988. *The Listening Ebony: Moral Knowledge, Religion, and Power among the Uduk of Sudan*. Oxford: Clarendon Press.

———. 1990. "Kings, Commoners, and the Ethnographic Imagination in Sudan and Ethiopia." In *Localizing Strategies*, ed. R. Fardon, 96–136. Edinburgh and Washington: Scottish Academic Press and Smithsonian Institution.

Jules-Rosette, B. 1975. *African Apostles*. Ithaca: Cornell University Press.

———. 1981. *Symbols of Change: Urban Transition in a Zambian Community*. Norwood, N.J.: Ablex.

Junod, Henry A. 1912. *The Life of a South African Tribe*. Neuchatel, Switzerland: Attinger Frères.

Kaberry, Phyllis. 1952. *Women of the Grassfields: A Study of the Economic Position of Women in Bamenda, British Cameroons*. London: Colonial Research Publications, no. 14. London: H. M. Stationery Office.

Kahn, Joel S., and Josep R. Llobera. 1980. "Towards a New Marxism or a New Anthropology." In *The Anthropology of Pre-Capitalist Societies*, ed. Kahn and Llobera, 263–29. London: Macmillan.

Kapferer, Bruce. 1972. *Strategy and Transaction in an African Society*. Manchester: Manchester University Press.

———. 1976. "Introduction." In *Transaction and Meaning: Directions in the Anthropology of Exchange and Symbolic Behavior*, ed. Kapferer, 1–24. ASA Essays, no. 1. Philadelphia: ISHI.

Karp, I. 1978. *Fields of Change*. London: Routledge and Kegan Paul.

Karp, I., and C. S. Bird, eds. 1980. *Explorations in African Systems of Thought*. Bloomington: Indiana University Press.

Kenyatta, Jomo. 1938. *Facing Mount Kenya*. London: Secker and Warburg.

Kopytoff, Igor. 1971. "Ancestors as Elders in Africa." *Africa* 41:129–42.

———. 1981. "The Authority of Ancestors." *Man* 16:135–37.

———, ed. 1987. *The African Frontier*. Bloomington: Indiana University Press.

Kroeber, A. 1931. "The Culture-Area and Age-Area Concepts of Clark Wissler." In *Methods in Social Science*, ed. S. Rice, 248–65. Chicago: University of Chicago Press.

Kuper, Adam. 1973. *Anthropologists and Anthropology: The British School, 1922–1972*. New York: Pica Press.

———. 1982. *Wives for Cattle*. London: Routledge and Kegan Paul.

Kuper, Hilda. 1947. *An African Aristocracy: Rank among the Swazi*. London: Oxford University Press.

———, ed. 1965. *Urbanization and Migration in West Africa*. Berkeley and Los Angeles: University of California Press.

Kuper, Leo, and M. G. Smith. 1969. *Pluralism in Africa*. Berkeley and Los Angeles: University of California Press.

Lackner, Helen. 1973. "Colonial Administration and Social Anthropology: Eastern Nigeria 1920–1940." In *Anthropology and the Colonial Encounter*, ed. Talal Asad, 123–51. London: Ithaca Press.

LaFontaine, J. S. 1977. "The Power of Rights." *Man* 12:421–37.

———. 1985. *Initiation: Ritual Drama and Secret Knowledge across the World*. Manchester: Manchester University Press.

Lan, David. 1985. *Guns and Rain: Guerillas and Spirit Mediums in Zimbabwe*. London: James Currey; Berkeley and Los Angeles: University of California Press.

Launay, R. 1982. *Traders without Trade: Responses to Change in Two Dyula Communities*. Cambridge: Cambridge University Press.

Leighton, Alexander, et al. 1963. *Psychiatric Disorder among the Yoruba*. Ithaca: Cornell University Press.

LeVine, Sarah. 1979. *Mothers and Wives*. Chicago: University of Chicago Press.

Lévi-Strauss, Claude. [1962] 1966. *The Savage Mind*. Chicago: University of Chicago Press.

———. [1955] 1974. *Tristes Tropiques*. New York: Atheneum.

Lévy-Bruhl, L. 1910. *Les fonctions mentales dans les sociétés inférieures*. Paris: Alcan.

References Cited

Lewis, I. M. 1961. *A Pastoral Democracy.* London: Oxford University Press.

——, ed. 1966 (reprinted 1980). *Islam in Tropical Africa.* Bloomington: Indiana University Press.

Lienhardt, Godfrey. 1976. "Social Anthropology of Africa." In *African Studies since 1945: a Tribute to Basic Davidson,* ed. Christopher Fyfe, 179–85. London: Longman.

Linares, Olga. 1992. *Power, Prayer, and Production: The Jola of Casamance, Senegal.* Cambridge: Cambridge University Press.

Little, K. 1965. *West African Urbanization.* Cambridge: Cambridge University Press.

——. 1973. *African Women in Towns: An Aspect of Africa's Social Revolution.* Cambridge: Cambridge University Press.

Lloyd, Peter C., ed. 1966. *The New Elites of Tropical Africa.* London: Oxford University Press for the International African Institute.

——. 1974. *Power and Independence: Urban Africans' Perceptions of Social Inequality.* London: Routledge and Kegan Paul.

Lloyd, Peter C., Akin L. Mabogunje, and B. Awe, eds. 1967. *The City of Ibadan.* Cambridge: Cambridge University Press.

Lubeck, P. 1986. *Islam and Urban Labor in Northern Nigeria: The Making of a Muslim Working Class.* Cambridge: Cambridge University Press.

McCall, Daniel F. 1967. "American Anthropology and Africa." *African Studies Bulletin* 10:20–34.

MacGaffey, J. 1987. *Entrepreneurs and Parasites: The Struggle for Indigenous Capitalism in Zaire.* New York: Cambridge University Press.

MacGaffey, Wyatt. 1981. "African Ideology and Belief." *African Studies Review* 24:227–74.

——. 1983. *Modern Kongo Prophets: Religion in a Plural Society.* Bloomington: Indiana University Press.

Mair, Lucy, ed. 1938. *Methods of Study of Culture Contact in Africa.* Memorandum no. 15. London: International African Institute.

——. 1962. *Primitive Government.* Bloomington: Indiana University Press.

Malinowski, Bronislaw. 1929. "Practical Anthropology." *Africa* 2:22–38.

——. 1930. "The Rationalization of Anthropology and Administration." *Africa* 3:405–30.

Mann, Kristin, and Richard Roberts, eds. 1991. *Law in Colonial Africa.* Portsmouth, N.H.: Heinemann Educational Books.

Marcus, George E., and Michael M. J. Fischer. 1986. *Anthropology as Cultural Critique.* Chicago: University of Chicago Press.

Mayer, Philip, and Iona Mayer. 1971. *Townsmen or Tribesmen: Conservatism and the Process of Urbanization in a South African City.* 2d ed. London: Oxford University Press.

Meek, C. K. 1925. *The Northern Tribes of Nigeria.* London: Oxford University Press.

———. 1931. *A Sudanese Kingdom.* London: K. Paul, Trench, Trubner.

———. 1937. *Law and Authority in a Nigerian Tribe.* London: Oxford University Press.

Meillassoux, Claude. 1960. "Essaie d'interpretation du phénomène économique dans les sociétés traditionelles d'autosubsistance." *Cahiers d'Études Africaines* 1:38–47.

———. 1964a. *Anthropologie économique des Gouro de Côte d'Ivoire.* Paris: Mouton.

———. 1964b. "Projet de recherche sur les systèmes économiques Africaines." *Journal de la Société des Africanistes* 34:292–98.

———. 1968. *Urbanization of an African Community: Voluntary Associations in Bamako.* American Ethnological Society Monographs, no. 45. Seattle: University of Washington Press.

———, ed. 1971. *The Development of Indigenous Trade and Markets in West Africa.* London: Oxford University Press.

———. 1981. *Maidens, Meal, and Money.* Cambridge and New York: Cambridge University Press.

———. [1975, in French] 1984. *Maidens, Meal, and Money.* Cambridge: Cambridge University Press.

Middleton, John. 1960. *Lugbara Religion.* London: Oxford University Press.

———. 1965. *Zanzibar: Its Society and Its Politics.* London: Oxford University Press for the Institute for Race Relations.

Middleton, John, and D. Tait. 1958. *Tribes without Rulers.* New York: Humanities Press; London: Routledge and Kegan Paul.

Miers, Suzanne, and Igor Kopytoff. 1977. *Slavery in Africa.* Madison: University of Wisconsin Press.

Miller, Christopher L. 1990. *Theories of Africans.* Chicago: University of Chicago Press.

Miner, Horace. 1953. *The Primitive City of Timbuctoo.* Princeton: Princeton University Press.

———, ed. 1967. *The City in Modern Africa.* New York: Praeger.

Mitchell, Clyde. 1956. *The Yao Village.* Manchester: Manchester University Press.

———. 1960. *Tribalism and the Plural Society.* London: Oxford University Press.

———. 1966. "Theoretical Orientations in African Urban Studies."

References Cited

In *The Social Anthropology of Complex Societies,* ed. Michael Banton, 37–68. London: Tavistock Publications.

———, ed. 1969. *Social Networks in Urban Situations.* Manchester: Manchester University Press for the Institute of Social Research, University of Zambia.

———. 1987. *Cities, Society, and Social Perception: A Central African Perspective.* Oxford: Oxford University Press.

Moore, Sally Falk. 1976. "The Secret of the Men." *Africa* 46:357–70.

———. 1978. "Archaic Law and Modern Times on the Zambezi." In *Cross-Examinations: Essays in Memory of Max Gluckman,* ed. Philip Gulliver, 53–77. Leiden: E. J. Brill.

———. 1986. *Social Facts and Fabrications: "Customary" Law on Kilimanjaro, 1880–1980.* Cambridge: Cambridge University Press.

———. 1987. "Explaining the Present: Theoretical Dilemmas in Processual Ethnography." *American Ethnologist* 14:727–36.

Morgan, Lewis Henry. [1877] 1963. *Ancient Society.* Cleveland and New York: Meridian Books.

Morrison, Minion K. C., and Peter C. W. Gutkind, eds. 1982. *Housing the Urban Poor in Africa.* Syracuse: Syracuse University Foreign and Comparative Studies/African Series.

Mudimbe, V. Y. 1988. *The Invention of Africa.* Bloomington: Indiana University Press.

Mullings, Leith. 1984. *Therapy, Ideology, and Social Change: Mental Healing in Urban Ghana.* Berkeley and London: University of California Press.

Murdock, George P. 1959. *Africa: Its Peoples and Their Culture History.* New York: McGraw Hill.

Murphee, M. W. 1969. *Christianity and the Shona.* London: Athlone.

Murray, Colin. 1981. *Families Divided: The Impact of Migrant Labor in Lesotho.* Cambridge: Cambridge University Press.

Nadel, S. F. 1942. *A Black Byzantium.* London: Oxford University Press.

———. 1954. *Nupe Religion.* London: Routledge.

———. 1967. *The Theory of Social Structure.* London: Oxford University Press.

Nolan, R. 1986. *Bassari Migrations: The Quiet Revolution.* Boulder, Col.: Westview.

Obbo, Christine. 1975. "Women's Careers in Low Income Areas as Indicators of County and Town Dynamics." In *Town and Country in Central and Eastern Africa,* ed. D. Parkin, 288–93. London: International African Institute.

———. 1980. *African Women: Their Struggle for Economic Independence.* London: Zed.

Oppong, Christine. 1974. *Marriage among a Matrilineal Elite: A Family Study of Ghanaian Senior Civil Servants.* Cambridge Studies in Social Anthropology, no. 8. Cambridge: Cambridge University Press.

———, ed. 1983. *Female and Male in West Africa.* London: Allen and Unwin.

Pan African Association of Anthropologists. Boite postale 1862, Yaounde: Cameroun.

Parkin, David. 1969. *Neighbors and Nationals in an African City Ward.* Berkeley and Los Angeles: University of California Press.

———. 1972. *Palms, Wine, and Witnesses.* San Francisco: Chandler.

———, ed. 1975. *Town and Country in East and Central Africa.* London: International African Institute.

———. 1978. *The Cultural Definition of Political Response.* London: Academic Press.

———. 1990. "Eastern Africa: The View from the Office and the Voice from the Field." In *Localizing Strategies,* ed. Richard Fardon, 182–203. Edinburgh and Washington: Scottish Academic Press and Smithsonian Institution Press.

———. 1991. *Sacred Void: Spatial Images of Work and Ritual among the Giriama of Kenya.* Cambridge: Cambridge University Press.

Parkin, David, and David Nyamwaya, eds. 1987. *Transformations of African Marriage.* Manchester: Manchester University Press for the International African Institute.

Parry, J., and M. Bloch, eds. 1989. *Money and the Morality of Exchange.* Cambridge: Cambridge University Press.

Paulme, Denise. 1960. *Women of Tropical Africa.* Berkeley and Los Angeles: University of California Press.

Peek, Philip M. 1990. "Japanese Anthropological Research on Africa." *African Studies Review* 33:93–131.

Peel, J. D. Y. 1968. *Aladura: A Religious Movement among the Yoruba.* London: Oxford University Press.

———. 1977. "Conversion and Tradition in Two African Societies: Ijebu and Buganda." *Past and Present* 77:108–41.

Pottier, Johan, ed. 1985. *Food Systems in Central and Southern Africa.* London: School of Oriental and African Studies.

———. 1988. *Migrants No More: Settlement and Survival in Mambwe Villages, Zambia.* Manchester: Manchester University Press for the International African Institute.

Rabinow, Paul. 1986. "Representations Are Social Facts: Modernity and Post-Modernity in Anthropology." In *Writing Culture,* ed. James Clifford and George Marcus, 234–61. Berkeley: University of California Press.

References Cited

Radcliffe-Brown, A. R. 1952. *Structure and Function in Primitive Society.* London: Cohen and West.

Radcliffe-Brown, A. R., and Daryll Forde, eds. 1950. *African Systems of Kinship and Marriage.* London: International African Institute, Oxford University Press.

Rattray, R. S. 1923. *Ashanti.* Oxford: Clarendon Press.

——. 1929. *Ashanti Law and Constitution.* Oxford: Clarendon Press.

Read, Margaret. 1938. *Native Standards of Living and African Culture Change, Illustrated by Examples from the Ngoni Highlands of Nyasaland.* London: Oxford University Press for the International Institute of African Languages and Cultures.

——. 1942. "Migrant Labor in Africa and Its Effects on Tribal Life." *International Labour Review* 45:605–31.

Redfield, Robert. 1941. *The Folk Culture of Yucatan.* Chicago: University of Chicago Press.

Rey, Pierre Philippe. 1969. "Articulation des modes de dépendance et des modes de reproduction dans deux sociétés lignageres (Punuet Kunyi du Congo-Brazzaville)." *Cahiers d'Etudes Africaines* 9:415–40.

——. 1971. *Colonialisme, neo-colonialisme, et transition au capitalisme.* Paris: Maspero.

——. 1973. *Les Alliances des Classes.* Paris: Maspero.

——. 1975. "The Lineage Mode of Production." *Critique of Anthropology* 3:27–79.

Richards, A. I. 1939. *Land, Labour, and Diet in Northern Rhodesia.* London: Oxford University Press.

——. 1940. *Bemba Marriage and Present Economic Conditions.* Rhodes-Livingstone Papers, no. 4. Livingstone, Northern Rhodesia: Rhodes-Livingstone Institute.

——. 1955. *Economic Development and Tribal Change.* Cambridge: Heffer.

——. 1959. *East African Chiefs.* New York: Praeger; London: Faber.

——. 1967. "African Systems of Thought: An Anglo-French Dialogue." *Man* 2:286–98.

Richards, Paul. 1985. *Historical Atlas of Africa.* Harlow, England: Longman.

Riesman, Paul. 1977. *Freedom in Fulani Social Life: An Introspective Ethnography.* Chicago: University of Chicago Press.

Rigby, Peter, 1969. *Cattle and Kinship among the Gogo.* Ithaca: Cornell University Press.

——. 1981. "Pastors and Pastoralists: The Differential Penetration of Christianity among East African Cattle Herders." *Comparative Studies in Society and History* 23:96–129.

Riley, Bernard W., and David Brokensha. 1988. *The Mbeere of Kenya.* Lanham, Md., London: University Press of America for the Institute for Development Anthropology.

Robertson, A. F. 1987. *The Dynamics of Productive Relationships: African Share Contracts in Comparative Perspective.* Cambridge: Cambridge University Press.

Rorty, R. 1986. "The Contingency of Language." *London Review of Books* 17 April, 3–6.

Ruel, M. 1969. *Leopards and Leaders.* London: Tavistock.

Said, Edward W. 1979. *Orientalism.* New York: Random House.

Sanjek, Roger. 1983. "Female and Male Domestic Cycles in Urban Africa: The Adabraka Case." In *Female and Male in West Africa,* ed. C. Oppong, 330–43. London: Allen and Unwin.

——— . 1990a. "Maid Servants and Market Women's Apprentices in Adabraka." In *At Work in Homes: Household Workers in World Perspective,* ed. Roger Sanjek and Shellee Colen, 35–61. American Ethnological Society Monograph Series, no. 3. Washington, D.C.: American Anthropological Association.

——— . 1990b. "Urban Anthropology in the 1980s: A World View." *Annual Review of Anthropology* 19:151–86.

Sargent, Carolyn Fishel. 1989. *Maternity, Medicine, and Power.* Berkeley and Los Angeles: University of California Press.

Schapera, Isaac. 1928. "Economic Changes in South African Native Life." *Africa* 1:170–88.

——— . 1938. *A Handbook of Tswana Law and Custom.* London: Oxford University Press.

——— . 1940. *Married Life in an African Tribe.* London: Faber and Faber.

——— . 1947. *Migrant Labor and Tribal Life.* London: Oxford University Press.

——— . 1956. *Government and Politics in Tribal Societies.* London: Watts.

Schildkrout, Enid. 1981. "The Employment of Children in Kano." In *Child Work, Poverty, and Underdevelopment,* ed. G. Rogers and G. Standing, 81–112. Geneva: International Library Office.

——— . 1983. "Dependence and Autonomy: The Economic Activities of Secluded Hausa Women in Kano." In *Female and Male in West Africa,* ed. C. Oppong, 107–26. London: Allen and Unwin.

——— . 1986a. "Children as Entrepreneurs: Case Studies from Kano." In *Entrepreneurship and Social Change,* ed. S. Greenfield and A. Strickon, 195–223. Lanham, Md.: University Press of America.

——. 1986b. "Widows in Hausa Society: Ritual Phase or Social Status." In *Widows in African Societies: Choices and Constraints,* ed. B. Potash, 131–52. Stanford, Calif.: Stanford University Press.

Schott, Rudiger. 1982. "Main Trends in German Ethnological Jurisprudence and Legal Ethnology." *Journal of Legal Pluralism* 20:37–68.

Scudder, Thayer, and Elizabeth Colson. 1980. *Secondary Education and the Formation of an Elite: The Impact of Education on Gwembe District, Zambia.* New York: Academic Press.

Seligman, C. G. 1957. *Races of Africa.* 3d ed. London: Oxford University Press.

Seligman, C. G., and B. Z. Seligman. 1932. *A Survey of the Pagan Tribes of the Nilotic Sudan.* London: Routledge.

Shipton, Parker. 1988. "The Kenyan Land Tenure Reform." In *Land and Society in Contemporary Africa,* ed. R. E. Downs and S. P. Reyna, 91–135. Hanover, N. H., and London: University Press of New England.

——. 1989. *Bitter Money: Cultural Economy and Some African Meanings of Forbidden Commodities.* American Ethnological Society Monograph Series, no. 1. Washington, D.C.: American Anthropological Association.

——. 1990. "African Famines and Food Security: Anthropological Perspectives." *Annual Review of Anthropology* 19:353–94.

Smith, E. W., and A. Dale. 1920. *The Ila-speaking Peoples of Northern Rhodesia.* London: Macmillan.

Smith, M. G. 1955. *The Economy of the Hausa Communities of Zaria.* London: H. M. Stationery Office.

——. 1956. "On Segmentary Lineage Systems." *Journal of the Royal Anthropological Institute* 86:39–80.

——. 1960. *Government in Zazzau.* London: Oxford University Press.

——. 1974. *Corporations and Society.* London: Duckworth.

——. 1978. *The Affairs of Daura.* Berkeley and Los Angeles: University of California Press.

Smith, M. G., and Leo Kuper, eds. 1969. *Pluralism in Africa.* Berkeley and Los Angeles: University of California Press.

Snyder, Francis. 1981. *Capitalism and Legal Change.* New York: Academic Press.

Southall, Aidan. 1954. *Alur Society.* Cambridge: Cambridge University Press.

——. 1961. *Social Change in Modern Africa.* London: Oxford University Press for the International African Institute.

——. 1970. "The Illusion of Tribe." *Journal of African and Asian Studies* 5:28–50.

——, ed. 1973. *Urban Anthropology: Cross-Cultural Studies of Urbanization.* London: Oxford University Press.

——. 1983. "The Contribution of Anthropology to African Studies." *African Studies Review* 26:63–76.

——. 1988. "The Segmentary State in Africa and Asia." *Comparative Studies in Society and History.* 30:52–88.

Southall, Aidan W., and Peter C. W. Gutkind. 1956. *Townsmen in the Making.* Kampala: East African Institute of Social Research.

Southwold, Martin. 1960. *Bureaucracy and Chiefship in Buganda.* East African Studies, no. 14. London: Kegan Paul for the East African Institute of Social Research.

Spencer, P. 1965. *The Samburu.* London: Routledge and Kegan Paul.

——. 1973. *Nomads in Alliance.* London: Oxford University Press for the School of Oriental and African Studies.

Sperber, D. 1974. *Rethinking Symbolism.* Cambridge: Cambridge University Press.

Staniland, Martin. 1983. "Who Needs African Studies?" *African Studies Review* 26:77–97.

Stewart, Frank. 1977. *Fundamentals of Age-Group Systems.* London: Academic Press.

Stocking, George W. 1987. *Victorian Anthropology.* New York and London: Free Press, Macmillan.

Stoller, Paul. 1987. *In Sorcery's Shadow: A Memoir of Apprenticeship among the Songhai of Niger.* Chicago: University of Chicago Press.

Stoller, Paul, and C. Olkes. 1986. "Bad Sauce, Good Ethnography." *Cultural Anthropology* 1:336–52.

Swantz, Marja-Liisa. 1985. *Women in Development, a Creative Role Denied: The Case of Tanzania.* London: C. Hurst; New York: St. Martin's Press.

Talbot, D. Amaury. 1915. *Woman's Mysteries of a Primitive People (Ibibio).* London: Cassell.

——. 1923. *Life in Southern Nigeria.* London: Macmillan.

——. 1926. *Peoples of Southern Nigeria.* 4 vols. London: H. Milford.

——. 1932. *Tribes of the Niger Delta.* London: Sheldon Press.

Tambiah, Stanley Jeyaraja. 1990. *Magic, Science, Religion, and the Scope of Rationality.* Cambridge: Cambridge University Press.

Tempels, P. [1945] 1959. *Bantu Philosophy.* Paris: Présence Africaine.

Terray, Emmanuel. 1969a. *Le Marxisme devant les sociétés primitives.* Paris: Maspero.

——. 1969b. *L'Organisation sociale des Dida de Côte d'Ivoire.* Abidjan, Côte d'Ivoire: Annales de l'Université d'Abidjan, series F, book 1, part 2.

———. 1972. *Marxism and Primitive Societies*. New York: Monthly Review Press.

———. 1974. "Long-Distance Exchange and the Formation of the State: The Case of the Abron Kingdom of Gyaman." *Economy and Society* 3:315–45.

———. 1986. "Présentation" In *Afrique plurielle, Afrique actuelle*, by Alfred Adler et al., 9–11. Paris: Karthala.

Thomas, C. Northcote. 1913–14. *Report on the Ibo-Speaking Peoples of Nigeria*. London: Harrison and Sons.

Thornton, Robert. 1980. *Space, Time, and Culture among the Iraqw of Tanzania*. New York: Academic Press.

Tonkin, Elizabeth. 1990. "West African Ethnographic Traditions." In *Localizing Strategies: Regional Traditions of Ethnographic Writing*, ed. Richard Fardon, 137–51. Edinburgh and Washington, D.C.: Scottish Academic Press, and Smithsonian Institution Press.

Tuden, Arthur, and Leonard Plotnicov, eds. 1970. *Social Stratification in Africa*. New York: Free Press, Collier Macmillan.

Turner, Victor. 1957. *Schism and Continuity in an African Society*. New York: Humanities Press; Manchester: Manchester University Press.

———. 1967. *The Forest of Symbols: Aspects of Ndembu Ritual*. Ithaca: Cornell University Press.

———. 1968. *The Drums of Affliction: A Study of Religious Processes among the Ndembu of Zambia*. Oxford: Clarendon Press and the International African Institute.

———. 1975. *Revelation and Divination in Ndembu Ritual*. Ithaca and London: Cornell University Press.

Tylor, Sir Edward Burnett. [1871] 1958. *Primitive Culture*. 2 vols. New York: Harper Torchbooks.

Van Binsbergen, W. M., and P. Geschiere, eds. 1985. *Old Modes of Production and Capitalist Encroachment: Anthropological Explorations in Africa*. London and New York: Kegan Paul International.

Van der Geest, Sjaak, and Jon P. Kirby. 1992. "The Absence of the Missionary in African Ethnography, 1930–1965." *African Studies Review* 35:59–103.

Vaughan, Megan. 1991. *Curing their Ills: Colonial Power and African Illness*. Stanford, Calif.: Stanford University Press.

Vincent, Joan. 1982. *Teso in Transition: The Political Economy of Peasant and Class in East Africa*. Berkeley and Los Angeles: University of California Press.

———. 1990. *Political Anthropology.* Tucson: University of Arizona Press.

Voegelin, Erminie W. 1950. "Anthropology in American Universities." *American Anthropologist* 52:350–91.

Wagner, U. 1982. *Catching the Tourist: Women Handicraft Traders in Gambia.* Stockholm: Department of Anthropology, University of Stockholm.

Watson, William. 1958. *Tribal Cohesion in a Money Economy.* Manchester: Manchester University Press.

Weber, Max. 1962. *The City.* New York: Collier Books.

Werbner, Richard ed. 1977. *Regional Cults.* ASA Monographs, no. 16. London: Academic Press.

———, ed. 1982. *Land Reform in the Making: Tradition, Public Policy, and Ideology in Botswana.* London: Rex Collins.

———. 1984. "The Manchester School in South-Central Africa." *Annual Review of Anthropology* 13:157–85.

Willis, Roy. 1974. *Man and Beast.* New York: Basic Books.

Wilson, Godfrey. [1941–42] 1968. *An Essay on the Economics of Detribalization in Northern Rhodesia.* 2 parts. Rhodes-Livingstone Papers, nos. 5 and 6. Livingstone, Northern Rhodesia: Rhodes-Livingstone Institute.

Wilson, Godfrey, and Monica Wilson. [1945] 1968. *The Analysis of Social Change.* Cambridge: Cambridge University Press.

Wilson, Monica. 1952. *Good Company: A Study of Nyakyusa Age Villages.* London: Oxford University Press.

———. 1957. *Rituals of Kinship among the Nyakyusa.* London: Oxford University Press.

———. 1959. *Communal Rituals of the Nyakyusa.* London: Oxford University Press.

———. 1977. *For Men and Elders: Change in the Relations of Generations and of Men and Women among the Nyakyusa-Ngonde People, 1875–1971.* New York: Africana Publishing Co. for the International African Institute.

Wirth, Louis. 1938. "Urbanism as a Way of Life." *American Journal of Sociology* 44:1–24.

Wissler, Clark. 1917. *The American Indian: An Introduction to the Anthropology of the New World.* New York: D. C. McMurtrie.

Wyllie, R. 1980. *The Spirit Seekers: New Religious Movements in Southern Ghana.* Missoula, Mont.: Scholars Press.

Author Index

161

Author Index

Subject Index